Recent Doctoral Research in Economic History

STUDIES IN SOCIAL AND ECONOMIC HISTORY
Edited by Herman Van der Wee

Volume 21

Erik Aerts & Herman Van der Wee, eds.

Recent Doctoral Research in Economic History

D-sessions

Proceedings
Tenth International Economic History Congress
Leuven, August 1990
Erik Aerts, General Editor

Leuven University Press
1990

Krakenstraat 3, B-3000 Leuven (Belgium)

ISBN 90 6186 393 7
D / 1990 / 1869 / 42

Cover: WKW Design Department Antwerp 90

CONTENTS

Modern Period

PREFACE

Organizers of world congresses in economic history have tried to incorporate new directions in the discipline and to encourage the discussion of new hypotheses. This special attention to what is new is also aimed at getting the younger generations of economic historians involved in the congresses. From Copenhagen in 1974, where the successful formula of informal workshops was introduced, their participation has especially been stimulated.

With the launch of the D-sessions at the Leuven congress in August 1990 the active participation of younger scholars will finally be built systematically into the programme. Every afternoon around five o'clock there will be parallel sessions for the ancient and medieval, early modern and modern periods at which young scholars who have just received their doctorates can put the results of their research to the world community of economic historians. The best doctoral theses will be awarded prizes of the International Economic History Association. This initiative of the International Association was warmly welcomed : more than forty entries from all over the world were received. From these twenty-four were selected for presentation at the congress.

We can make a few general remarks on the basis of the scope and content of the submissions. One immediate conclusion is that the distribution across periods was very uneven. Only a few theses dealt with the ancient and medieval periods; those for the early modern period were a bit more numerous, but still fairly few. On the other hand, there is a vast interest in the modern period, the subject of the great majority of the submissions. The topics dealt with in the submissions are closely related to current fashions : the early modern theses focus on demographic and agrarian history; those for the modern period on industrial and technological history. Methodologically the picture is traditional. The quantitative element is important, but remains mainly descriptive : cliometrics does not seem to have made a major breakthrough. Social anthropology has an influence on the early modern theses. Micro-economics and business history leave a clear impression on the modern theses.

The organizers of the D-sessions hope that the initiative will be continued in future congresses and that more young scholars will offer to present their research for discussion in these sessions. They also hope the interest shown in their work will lead younger generations to innovate and to broaden their research both thematically and methodologically.

We cannot close without a word of thanks to all those who have contributed to the organization of the D-sessions in Leuven : the Executive Committee of the International Association, which approved of our initiative; the colleagues who have taken responsibility for the selection of participants (Rondo Cameron, Aldo de Maddalena and Jerzy Topolski for the ancient and medieval period; Akira Hayami, Peter Klein and Paul Pach for the early modern period; Alexander Fursenko, Lennart Jörberg and Peter Mathias for the modern period); Peter Solar as congress coordinator; Raymond Doms, Edward Haasl and Micheline Soenen for their help in improving the English and French of some texts; and last but not least Erik Aerts, who accepted the time-consuming and delicate task of editing the manuscripts.

Herman Van der Wee
President
International Economic History Association

De Hettinghe, September 1989

NOTE ON THE TRANSLATIONS

All the authors were asked to supply a text in English or French. We appreciate the difficulties involved in preparing such summaries in a language apart other than one's own but consider that the importance of the content justifies the effort. When linguistic editing seemed appropriate, we did so as far as our finances and the time available permitted. Changes were made only with the approval of the authors, and care was taken not to alter the substance of an argument. Indeed, we consider the richness of the different scholarly traditions brought together in this Symposium to be one of its primary benefits. The expression of that richness is difficult, we realize, so we ask the reader's indulgence for the occasional lapses in standard syntax.

Erik Aerts
General Editor
Proceedings Tenth International
Economic History Congress Leuven

ANTIQUITY & MIDDLE AGES

RECHERCHES SUR L'ECONOMIE APULIENNE AU IIe ET AU Ier SIECLE AVANT NOTRE ERE

PHILIPPE DESY

A l'exception de la Campanie, l'Italie du sud d'après Hannibal est le plus souvent décrite d'une manière extrêmement pessimiste dans les grandes synthèses d'histoire économique. Ruinée et dépeuplée par la deuxième guerre punique, cette région serait devenue la proie des grands propriétaires romains qui y auraient introduit et encouragé une économie esclavagiste basée sur une transhumance dévastatrice des troupeaux ou, au mieux, sur une céréaliculture extensive. L'objet de cette thèse est, suivant le conseil exprimé par C. Nicolet, *Les structures de l'Italie romaine* (Paris, 1977), d'étudier une région particulière de manière approfondie, tant sur le plan des sources écrites que des données archéologiques, pour vérifier le fondement de cette vision moderne. L'Apulie présentait des avantages évidents pour une telle recherche : elle est tenue par plusieurs historiens contemporains pour l'exemple même de zone 'sous-développée' en Italie méridionale, mais ses spécificités archéologiques y sont tout à fait particulières, et sous-exploitées par les chercheurs.

Une introduction géographique insiste sur la diversité du paysage apulien. L'analyse des caractéristiques de chaque secteur montre que l'élevage des moutons, attesté par plusieurs sources, peut avoir été limité à des zones spécifiques, naturellement peu peuplées, sans qu'il faille y voir une conséquence directe de la deuxième guerre punique; la présumée 'révolte des bergers' (ou des adeptes de Bacchus?) de 185 pose d'ailleurs trop de problèmes au niveau de l'analyse des sources et du commentaire économique pour étayer des hypothèses. En revanche, l'importance des relations maritimes entre la Méditerranée orientale et l'Apulie, en particulier dans la péninsule Sallentine qui est extrêmement riche en ports au sud de Brindes et de Tarente, fait présager de l'existence d'économies plus complexes.

L'implication de l'Apulie dans la deuxième guerre punique est étudiée dans le détail des événements, avec plusieurs mises au point de chronologie et de commentaires dans les récits de Polybe et de Tite-Live. Bien qu'il ne soit pas permis de mettre en doute la gravité des dévastations causées par cette guerre, on relève que l'ensemble de l'Apulie rurale est alors restée en mesure de ravitailler les importantes armées carthaginoise et romaines qui ont séjourné et combattu sur son territoire entre 217 et 207; il est donc totalement exclu de souscrire à l'hypothèse de massacres systématiques des populations. Dès lors, il n'y a plus aucune raison de s'étonner de ce que le Sénat ait fait acheter (*coemere*) en Apulie et dans le Sallentin le blé nécessaire à l'expédition de Grèce en 172 (LIV. 42, 27, 8). Quant au problème des terres confisquées par les Romains et transférées à *l'ager publicus* en guise de représailles, il pose en Apulie des questions insurmontables en raison des contradictions de nos sources.

Dans la description géographique de Strabon, la remise des données dans leur contexte impliquait un passage par la 'Quellenforschung'. Au terme du détour qu'imposait cette démarche, l'acquis a été aisé à synthétiser : les visions de l'Apulie qu'avaient les deux grandes sources de l'Amaséen, Artémidore d'Ephèse et Poseidonios d'Apamée, sont, du point de vue de l'économie rurale et marchande, fort favorables. Une phrase pessimiste que l'on trouve dans le traité, qui expose que l'Apulie, autrefois florissante, fut désolée 'par la guerre d'Hannibal et par celles qui suivirent' (STRABON 6, 3, 11) apparaît, dans son imprécision et sa contradiction (seul le nord de l'Apulie fut, en raison de son caractère osque, touché par la guerre sociale), comme une digression personnelle d'un Strabon inspiré par Polybe, et il est difficile d'accorder à cette incise un crédit identique à celui que mérite l'ensemble du chapitre 6,3. Ce type de démarche revêt une certaine importance tant il apparaît que les préjugés défavorables à l'Apulie que l'on retrouve dans nombre d'ouvrages actuels reposent sur un petit nombre de clichés lesquels, replacés dans leur contexte, perdent de leur importance; c'est notamment le cas du jeu de mots *Apulia*-ἀπόλλυμι (PAUL, *Historia Langobardorum* 2, 21) et de l'*inanissima pars Italiae* de Cicéron (*Att.* 8, 3).

L'analyse du traité d'économie rurale de Varron, bien que revêtant une importance fondamentale, a été aisée et confortante : dans un passage dont l'interprétation doit s'accorder avec la traduction proposée par J. Heurgon contre les attaques successives de J. Kolendo, Varron (*Rr* 1, 29, 2) tient les emblavures *non tam latae* – relativement petites –, ainsi que la céréaliculture intensive, pour typiques de l'Apulie; il nous apporte aussi divers renseignements sur le vin et l'huile, dont Caton permet de penser que la production avait déjà commencé vers la fin du IIIe siècle en Apulie du sud, probablement sous l'influence de Tarente. Ces produits seront encore mentionnés par Horace dont, à l'analyse, on ne peut que louer la justesse des détails de nature économique.

La conclusion de l'analyse approfondie des sources littéraires sur l'Apulie amène à penser qu'une partie de ce territoire devait être divisée en domaines de dimensions relativement restreintes, bien mis en valeur par des cultures de blé *triticum* dont la qualité était renommée et d'arbres fruitiers, dans le cadre d'entreprises familiales assistées par des travailleurs saisonniers, où les esclaves ne constituaient pas la majorité de la main-d'œuvre.

Il eût été souhaitable d'étayer cette conclusion au moyen d'une documentation archéologique classique, reposant par exemple sur des fouilles de villas. Malheureusement, en la matière, seul un rapide exposé de la situation a été autorisé car ce type de recherche n'a pas été suffisamment préparé pour l'Apulie républicaine – peut-être est-ce d'ailleurs le cas de l'ensemble de l'Italie, l'*ager Cosanus* et certains secteurs de la Campanie exceptés. En Apulie méridionale, aucune découverte archéologique de ce type n'aurait pu fournir d'argument précis pour la thèse, trop circonscrite dans le temps. En Apulie septentrionale, la situation est plus complexe car un certain nombre de villas y ont été reconnues et même fouillées; elles confirment la présence d'exploitations impliquées dans la production de l'huile, mais leur existence couvre naturellement des périodes fort longues. De plus, des reconnaissances par photographies aériennes effectuées voici plus de quarante ans par J. Bradford et brièvement republiées par G.B.D. Jones, *ArchClass* 32 (1983), 85-100, confirment qu'une partie importante du Tavoliere fut centurié et mis en valeur par l'intermédiaire d'exploitations moyennes évaluées au maximum à cent *iugera.* Mais la date de la mise en place de ce réseau manque d'arguments tout à fait convaincants.

Les amphores commerciales constituent l'un des matériaux les plus originaux mis en œuvre dans la thèse. Elles confirment d'une façon indéniable que l'Apulie méridionale, à partir d'une date que l'on ne peut faire remonter haut dans le IIe siècle, exporta dans des conteneurs de formes nouvelles (amphores de Brindes et, en partie, Lamboglia 2 et Dressel 2-4) de l'huile d'olive, mais aussi du vin. Il ne s'agissait pas, surtout en ce qui concerne ce dernier produit, d'une innovation, mais plutôt d'une insertion dans des échanges attestés en Italie tyrrhénienne depuis une période bien antérieure; mais la caractéristique de notre commerce apulien semble avoir été sa direction plus orientale, notamment vers Délos et l'Egypte; l'examen de cette dernière région constitue une réelle nouveauté, aucun document papyrologique ne faisant état d'importations d'huile ou de vins italiens à une époque aussi haute. Ce commerce dut connaître des moments très favorables sous la dictature d'un Sylla qui privilégia les activités de Brindes. La thèse attribuerait la diminution, très sensible, de la production de ces amphores apuliennes, au blocage des ports de Brindes, de Tarente et de Siponte pendant les guerres civiles inaugurées en 49, plus qu'aux conséquences de la chute du commerce des esclaves selon le modèle présenté par A. Tchernia, *Le vin de l'Italie romaine* (Paris, 1986), pp. 68-74.

Mais les amphores apuliennes, en particulier du type de Brindes, présentent la caractéristique d'être fréquemment timbrées. Ce matériel épigraphique est d'une richesse d'autant plus insoupçonnée qu'il est peu ou non encore publié. Il a dès lors nécessité la constitution d'un catalogue d'inscriptions le plus complet possible et fort original puisqu'il comporte nombre d'inédits rassemblés en Italie méridionale mais aussi dans d'autres secteurs sous-exploités comme l'Albanie. Ont été ainsi recensées environ deux mille anses sur lesquelles ont été reconnus, après diverses améliorations dans les lectures et plusieurs tentatives de classement aidées par ordinateur, 42 noms d'entrepreneurs (parmi lesquels un homme de confiance de Sylla) et 160 noms d'esclaves-potiers. L'analyse de cette documentation a amené à conclure que les amphores brindisines ont été façonnées dans leur majorité sous la direction d'entrepreneurs qui n'étaient pas des propriétaires terriens, et se limitaient au plus à faire transporter jusqu'aux ports les produits alimentaires évoqués par Varron dans un passage où est justement prise comme exemple la zone de Brindes (*Rr* 2, 6, 5).

La reconstitution proposée va donc quelque peu à l'encontre de la théorie latifondiaire (un terme dont l'usage a d'ailleurs été refusé dans la thèse car il ne saurait s'appliquer à la période concernée), à laquelle souscrivent volontiers plusieurs savants actuels par la généralisation du cas des timbres amphoriques cosans de Sestius. Le problème de la capacité de domaines aux dimensions moyennes à s'insérer dans une économie de marché n'est plus gênant depuis que W. Kula a montré tout le schématisme qu'il y aurait à opposer un 'secteur commercialisé' et un 'secteur de subsistance'; dans la réalité des faits, il devait être plus aisé à de petits propriétaires d'exporter leurs surplus qu'à des 'latifondiaires' que leurs frais auraient empêchés de vendre au-delà d'un certain seuil. D'autre part, les producteurs d'amphores de Brindes ne paraissent pas non plus pouvoir être rangés dans la catégorie des *negotiatores* du fait que leurs noms ne sont jamais signalés dans les inscriptions de Délos.

Les amphores nous ont réservé une autre confirmation des textes : en face de l'Apulie rurale qui aurait répondu au principe de la concurrence parfaite et aurait donc été exclusivement exportatrice à l'époque qui nous intéresse, Tarente a bien été, de manière constante et malgré la concurrence croissante de Brindes, une place au trafic appréciable où l'on achetait des vins originaires de partout. Or, selon Artémidore d'Ephèse, source probable de Strabon, la colonie de Caius Gracchus aurait eu des effets positifs sur la vie tarentine, et Cicéron puis Horace vantèrent les aspects épicuriens de cette métropole.

Il serait dès lors excessif de considérer que l'Apulie des IIe et Ier siècles avant notre ère se serait uniquement caractérisée par l'extension de ses propriétés, suite ultime des confiscations successives aux alliances avec Hannibal, ou par la faible mise en valeur de son sol. Cette conclusion va donc à l'encontre des idées développées dans les grands manuels économiques de M. Rostovtzeff ou de T. Frank, mais aussi des synthèses plus récentes d'A.J. Toynbee ou de P.A. Brunt; le dernier avatar de ces reconstitutions serait une théorie énoncée par A. Carandini et divers chercheurs de l'Institut Gramsci lors du congrès de 1979 *Società romana e produzione schiavistica* (Rome/Bari, 1981); leur schéma oppose une Italie tyrrhénienne parvenue à un stade de développement 'pré-industriel' avec une spécialisation dans la culture de la vigne à une Apulie, comparable aux pays actuellement en marge de l'expansion industrielle, pourvoyeuse en céréales de ces régions développées.

Le matériel étudié dans la thèse ne corrobore pas ce modèle, non seulement dans le cas de l'Apulie, mais aussi dans celui de l'ensemble de la façade adriatique italienne dont il apparaît avec une certitude tout à fait actuelle qu'elle fut largement impliquée dans l'exportation du vin. Toutefois, en dépit de l'apparente similitude de certains faits, l'intention de la thèse n'est pas d'étendre à l'ensemble de l'Italie la vision proposée d'une partie de l'Apulie divisée en domaines familiaux petits ou moyens, car les amphores ont permis d'énoncer une nouvelle mise en garde. Au IIe siècle, l'apparition tardive des conteneurs apuliens par rapport aux tyrrhéniens suppose en effet que les agriculteurs apuliens se sont insérés dans un marché déjà organisé, avec les lenteurs habituelles des réactions de l'agriculture face à l'évolution de la demande. En d'autres termes, si les produits étaient apuliens, l'initiative commerciale, elle, ne l'était pas, du moins au départ.

Aussi, l'apparente incapacité du commerce des amphores apuliennes à se ressaisir après les tourmentes des guerres civiles ne surprendra plus depuis qu'A. Tchernia a constaté que les cépages qui ont le mieux franchi ce cap bénéficiaient de protections ou de capitaux extérieurs, dont les investissements sénatoriaux sont la forme la plus évidente. Ces investissements semblent avoir manqué en Apulie, ce qui expliquerait l'appauvrissement de cette région sous le Haut-Empire, caractéristique qui, jusqu'à présent, a trop souvent été appliquée à l'Apulie de la fin de la période républicaine.

URBANISM AND UNDERDEVELOPMENT: ROMAN POMPEII

WILLEM JONGMAN

No modern tourist can fail to be impressed by the ruins of ancient Pompeii. Its large private homes are often decorated with fine wallpaintings, the beauty of which is apparent even after the damage and neglect of modern times. A visit to the museum in Naples, where most movable objects are held, adds further emphasis to an already overwhelming impression of sumptuous wealth. At least as impressive as the private wealth, however, are public amenities such as theatres, public baths and water supplies, or the paved streets. Those had not been cheap.

Roman urbanism was impressive. The level of urbanization in core areas of the empire such as Italy was high by pre-industrial standards. The city of Rome, with a population of perhaps one million inhabitants in the first century A.D., is unmatched in European pre-industrial history. But even apart from Rome, urbanization was high, and it may be estimated that at least a quarter, and more likely a third, of the Italian population of the first century A.D. lived in its more than 400 cities. Rome was an urban society, and Roman urbanism exceeds nearly everything in European pre-industrial history. That is important, because urbanization is often used as an index of development.

The private homes were large, and many Pompeians lived in such houses. Unfortunately for them, that was often as domestic slaves. The construction and operation of splendid public facilities was made possible in part by the low cost of labour. Social inequality was large; many lived at or near subsistence, and life expectancy was low. If we look at it over a longer period of time, we can say that the last one or two centuries B.C. and the first two centuries A.D. probably witnessed a larger total output than the period before or after. The standard of living of the mass of the population, however, remained very low, and there is no evidence for an improvement over the centuries of Roman imperial history. Ultimately, the Roman Empire fell. It fell because its economy was hard-pressed to support the necessary military expense, and because its elite quite successfully avoided the burden.

Roman economic development thus presents an ambiguous picture, and it need, therefore, not surprise us that scholars hold strongly divergent views. The publication in 1973 of Sir Moses Finley's *The Ancient Economy* (London, 1985^{2}) has been a watershed in this debate. In this work a full scale attack is launched on prevailing views about the nature of the ancient economy and on accepted methodologies. Finley argued that it was wrong to apply modern concepts such as those from modern economic theory to the study of the ancient world. This was wrong because the ancient world was not an integrated market economy; instead, its economy was 'embedded' in the rest of society. This entails that much economic behaviour was governed by the value-systems of social groups, and not so much by some economic rationality. In the ancient world, landowners, whether working farmers or gentlemen land-owners, were the core of the citizenry. The mass of the population worked in agriculture, and even though the elite normally lived in the cities, its income was overwhelmingly of agricultural origin. The dominant value system could find little attraction in commerce and industry. No commercial bourgeoisie emerged, and, therefore, the ancient economy did not grow. Ancient cities were consumer cities, rather than producer cities. Here, Finley follows scholars of an earlier generation such as Werner Sombart and Max Weber who had viewed the commercial bourgeoisie of later centuries as the embodiment of a new kind of economically rational behaviour, and responsible for economic innovation and growth.

Criticism of the Finley model has largely focussed on providing counter examples of (mostly indirect) elite involvement in urban commerce and industry, accompanied by suggestions that those sectors of the ancient economy were not as underdeveloped as Finley had suggested. Much (though obviously not all) of this criticism is empirically wrong, or of insufficient consequence. It is interesting, however, that critics have continued to accept Finley's rejection of the use of modern economic theory, and have agreed with him that the presence of a commercial bourgeoisie with concomitant entrepreneurial rationalism and exporting 'producer cities' are universal indices of economic development.

In my *The Economy and Society of Pompeii* (Amsterdam, 1988) I argue that the rejection of modern economic theory is mistaken.

Economic theory does not make the modernizing assumptions which are alleged. Economically rational behaviour is not a historical phenomenon, the emergence of which can be used to explain economic innovation. I also argue that the ancient historians' yardstick for successful economic development (medieval and early modern history) has been misinterpreted. Recent research in those fields has begun to question seriously the importance of urbanization and the commercial bourgeoisie as engines for growth. Research emphasis among economic and social historians of antiquity has, therefore, been misdirected.

Town-country relations, then, are crucial for the debate on the ancient economy and for an understanding of ancient social structure. For nearly all individual ancient cities the evidence is pitiful, however. Apart from exceptional cities such as Athens or Rome, one city stands out as a potential candidate for a case study : Pompeii. It is, moreover, not infrequently quoted as an example of ancient producer cities. Buried under the thick layers of volcanic ashes from Vesuvius' eruption in A.D. 79, it gives the ancient historian the nearest thing to a time-capsule. Even if a sample of one can, of course, never be representative, we could have fared worse in this respect. It is an Italian site of the first century A.D., and in that sense it represents Roman urbanism at its most impressive : this is the area where and the period when we would expect it to be most highly developed. With its 8000-12,000 inhabitants (within the walls) it was probably bigger than most Roman towns – but it was no metropolis. The Pompeian territory is very fertile, and population density was well above the Italian average. In studying Pompeii we study Roman urbanism under a magnifying glass. A small later provincial town (perhaps more representative for the average ancient city than Pompeii) would be a less likely candidate as a producer city. I shall argue that even in its most developed form as in Pompeii, the Roman city was no producer city.

This is not to say, however, that there are no problems with the Pompeian time-capsule. The unique top layer of the site provides abundant data for the most recent history of the town. The lower layers, however, are not at all privileged compared to other sites. This, and a justified hesitation to damage the surface layer for excavation of lower levels, have had the effect that, compared to other sites, there is an enormous wealth of information for one period, and little for the period before (or, naturally, for the period after A.D. 79). The consequence is that, unfortunately, Pompeii is unsuitable for dynamic analysis : it is a necessarily static cross-section at more or less one moment in time (albeit an important moment).

But the chronological concentration of the data is not the only sense in which Pompeian data are unique. The specific conditions of conservation have preserved whole types of data for us which have not (or hardly) survived at other sites. The archive of writing tablets that will figure so prominently in my statistical analysis on the dimensions of social inequality is near unique, and is certainly far larger and more homogeneous than anything from elsewhere. This is also true for the thousands of posters with electoral propaganda and, in a different way, for the extent of surviving housing. Other data, however, are conspicuous by their absence. Inscriptions on stone, in particular public ones, are few in number. Though many villa sites have survived, their interpretation is hampered by the impossibility of normal field surveys : the layer of ash is too thick to yield many surface finds. The unique composition of the evidence poses methodological problems : we cannot rely much on our experience from other sites to interpret the data. All too easily we may make the mistake of using the same data both to formulate our hypotheses and to validate them. I have tried to employ two strategies to combat the problem. Firstly, I have always looked with one eye to the world outside Pompeii, and preferred that as a source of hypotheses and a potential control. Secondly, I have preferred to concentrate on a more formal analysis of larger and more or less serial data sets. That should constrain and control speculation at least to some extent.

The population and total production of the Roman empire were large. In chapter two ('introducing the problem') I elaborate on this point, in part with further theoretical analysis. In good economic fashion I begin with an analysis of demand and supply in Roman Italy. I argue that food plays a major role in both, and that at prevailing high levels of population density, producing enough food required a major effort. Such intensive agriculture requires large labour inputs, and inevitably labour productivity will be low. This was all the more so since the lack of good pasture-land militated heavily against a large-scale use of working animals. In that sense the history of mediterranean agriculture is different from that in more northern areas.

The problems and possibilities of increasing agricultural output to feed growing numbers of people have long been a field of economic reflection. In recent years the work of Ester Boserup has drawn attention to the possibilities of more frequent cropping to achieve a higher productivity of the land; but the other side of the coin is that under traditional conditions that requires a disproportionate increase in labour input, with low labour productivity (and, therefore, a declining standard of living) as a result. Elaborating on this analysis, Jan de Vries has argued that specialization between town and country may alleviate this. Whereas under traditional conditions population pressure is responsible for the fragmentation of holdings and increased dependence of impoverished peasants on big landowners, specialization may avert these evils. Then the peasantry may remain relatively strong and independent, and the urban elite can be a commercial and manufacturing elite, rather than one of landowners resident in towns. What happened in Roman Italy?

Chapter three ('agriculture') takes the argument into Pompeii, and is focussed in particular on its agriculture. The traditional view of Pompeian agriculture emphasizes the production for external markets of cash crops such as wine and olive oil. I argue that it is mistaken. It ignores the prominence of cereal agriculture in literary sources about Campania, and is naive in its implicit conviction that the surviving archeological evidence for villa agriculture can be extrapolated to parts of the territory for which no such evidence exists. I argue that where traces of villa agriculture are absent, there were no villas in antiquity. Instead, I posit small (and probably more or less dependent) peasants concentrating on cereal agriculture.

I then offer three efforts at validation of my hypothesis. The first of these is that it appears no coincidence that the villas are where they are: their location coincides with what one would predict from location theory. The second validation comes in the form of an effort to calculate aggregate supply of and demand for food in the town and its territory. The traditional view of Pompeian agriculture never bothered about the origin of the grain that was needed to feed the population, nor did it ever consider whether the quantity of wine likely to have been produced was large enough to leave a major surplus for export. My tentative calculations indicate that the traditional view is improbable : the wine surplus would be non-existent and a large area would be necessary to grow enough cereals. The third effort at validation consists of a comparison with early-modern Campania. It is reassuring (even if no proof) to note that, in that period too, the area was devoted to cereal agriculture. This comparison with later times permits a more detailed analysis of the logic of the very intensive agriculture in the area. Population density was so high (and roughly equal to that in antiquity) that production per hectare had to be very high as well. The result was that labour productivity was low : the standard of living of the working population was appalling. A higher labour productivity would have been possible if working animals had replaced some of the human labour. Inevitably population density would have been lower, however : the food requirements of the animals would not have permitted the high prevailing population density.

Chapter four ('urban manufacturing, the textile industry') concerns the urban economy : can we find evidence for major manufacturing for external markets, that the urban elite was substantially involved in this, that it was not just a group of landowners resident in town? I have chosen to concentrate on the one branch of industry that constitutes a decisive test : the textile industry. If medieval and early-modern cities develop a substantial exporting industry (often enough they do not) it almost invariably concerns textiles, and it has been argued that this was so in Pompeii.

That is, however, wrong. Of course there were textile workshops, but there is nothing to suggest that their scale exceeded the requirements of the local market. Neither is there any evidence to validate the view that the Pompeian fullers fulfilled a coordinating entrepreneurial role for the entire industry, or that the elite were directly involved. Pompeian industry was not heavily concentrated on one particular industry (textiles), but was very differentiated. This suggests production for a sophisticated local demand, rather than for export.

Elite income and expenditure seem important to understand the ancient city. Therefore, in chapter five ('epilogue'), we leave the confines of Pompeii. After a brief critical review of Hopkins' 'Taxes and Trade' model for the economy of Roman towns, I propose a tentative model to relate elite income and expenditure and its place in the Italian economy of the early Empire. Already a very conservative estimate of elite income and its purchasing power (in multiples of bare annual subsistence needs for one person) demonstrates that it would be enough to keep the economy of Italian towns fully occupied. The coincidence between the number of people that could be fed on estimated elite consumer spending and the actual number of urban residents in Italy is remarkable. Conversely – assuming an agricultural origin for elite income – the number of people necessary in agriculture to produce this income amounts to nearly the entire rural population of Italy. Although this model – deliberately and perhaps unjustifiably – ignores the additional income from imperialism, it still is a novel corroboration of the 'consumer city' thesis and its emphasis on the social relations between town and country.

The second half of the chapter then returns to the question of the nature of Roman economic development and its potential for further growth. I conclude that the economic specialization between town and country was of only limited importance. Urbanism in itself was not enough for commercialization. The Pompeian economy is a good example of a traditional economy driven very hard, rather then of a transformation of the production function. Treading water at this level could provide many impressive examples of urbanism and sophistication, even if the benefits accrued mostly to a small elite. It was a situation, however, in which the road to further growth was blocked precisely by the mechanisms which had allowed it to get where it got.

If, so far, the emphasis has been on the economic aspects of Pompeian society, this is different in the rest. Social inequality and subordination are important if we want to understand the nature of ancient economic performance. The argument about the relative scarcity of factors of production should be reflected in an inequality between people : some only have their labour to offer, and should, therefore, not expect a high standard of living (given low labour productivity). The really scarce factor was land. Therefore, ownership of land marks the 'haves' from the 'have nots'. Nearly all Pompeian land was probably controlled by the elite. That, unfortunately, is about as far as we can take speculation about rural social relations in Pompeii. The urban evidence (which fortunately also refers to rural Pompeii at times) allows far more possibilities. The first question which concerns us is whether or not a social group with some of the characteristics of a bourgeoisie emerged. Did social mobility change the nature of the elite, or was it only renewal without structural change? The second question concerns the ideological cohesion of society. Was the elite able to impose acceptance of prevailing inequality, and how could that be so? We shall, in other words, be concerned not only with social structure as a reflection of economic inequalities, but also with the social potential for structural transformation of economic relations.

The 'dimensions of social inequality' take the central stage in chapter six. Using the order in which the witnesses signed the documents in the famed archive of writing tablets from the banker L. Caecilius Iucundus, I have reconstructed a hierarchy of prestige positions which is, I suggest, representative of Pompeian society. What, however, makes some end up at the top, and others at the bottom? To this end I made a statistical comparison between this prestige ordening, and other dimensions of inequality. I argue that even if wealth is a necessary condition for prestige, it is demonstrably not sufficient. Traditional requirements such as free birth and office-holding must be fulfilled before wealth can be transformed into prestige. Getting rich quickly (as may be possible in trade) is not enough. Anticipatory socialization towards elite values and modes of behaviour (such as landownership) is necessary – as is patience. Social risers (such as wealthy freedmen) have to transform themselves in order to be accepted. Social mobility does not transform social structure, but only renews the elite. No bourgeoisie could emerge.

Chapter seven then takes these problems into the area of 'power and obligation'. The wealth of Pompeian electoral propaganda has suggested to some that political participation was substantial, and could lead to a transformation of the political elite and its behaviour. I shall argue, however, that Pompeii was not a bourgeois democracy. The language of the electoral propaganda suggests relations of patronage rather than opposition between social groups. How was the elite able to control the votes of the mass of the population at elections? I argue that voting procedure suggests that voting was governed by localized patronage networks. The landowning elite's ability to control was strong, and the electorate obliged. But how about social risers : could they obtain election? And more particularly, could social mobility seriously alter the values and behaviour of the elite so as to make it more amenable to the sort of economically innovative behaviour characteristic of the later bourgeoisie? I do not think so. The elite's power of control over aspiring candidates was strong, and support was conditional upon socialization. The need to conform was strong, and social mobility could, therefore, not be a challenge for transformation. The elite was renewed rather than transformed by the incorporation of newcomers.

REFERENCE

This paper reports the results of my *The Economy and Society of Pompeii* (Amsterdam : J.C. Gieben, 1988). The reader is referred to this publication for bibliography and further details.

ECONOMIE RURALE ET DEMOGRAPHIE EN FLANDRE PENDANT LE BAS MOYEN AGE ET LE DEBUT DES TEMPS MODERNES

Test-case : Les châtellenies d'Audenarde et d'Alost
(fin du XIIIe - première moitié du XVIe siècle)

ERIK THOEN*

BUT DES RECHERCHES

Notre étude (publiée en néerlandais; Thoen 1988) avait comme premier but d'analyser l'économie rurale de la Flandre pendant la période connue comme 'crise du bas Moyen Age' (XIVe-XVe siècles), considérée comme coupure cruciale dans l'historiographie. Notre intérêt s'est surtout orienté vers les mouvements longs et demi-longs de la conjoncture et vers la structure de l'économie. Le but final était d'élaborer un modèle explicatif situé dans un contexte international. Nous avons dû limiter le cadre géographique à une région représentative et bien documentée c.-à-d. le sud de la Flandre Orientale.

La majorité des études sur l'économie rurale de la Flandre au XIVe et XVe siècles – pour la plupart des articles de synthèse – ont emprunté aux articles de Van Uytven (1961) et de Van der Wee (1972) l'image d'une économie rurale peu touchée par la crise du bas Moyen Age. Certains ont même dénié l'existance d'une crise, sauf pour la fin du XVe siècle (E. Aerts-E. Van Cauwenberghe 1984). D'autres, comme Verhulst (1963) étaient plus 'pessimistes', surtout pour le XIVe siècle. Point de départ de notre étude était donc de vérifier ces thèses, de délimiter les phases et surtout de rechercher une explication pour cette différence eventuelle avec le 'modèle Européen'.

* chercheur qualifé du FNRS

L'EVOLUTION DE LA CONJONCTURE

Nous avons rassemblé des indices conjoncturelles – 'classiques' et 'non-classiques' – tels que les prix, les salaires, l'évolution démographique, mais aussi le niveau du prélèvement et des investissements, et couvrants une période aussi large que possible.

Une analyse comparée nous a révélé une vraie 'conjoncture', c.-à-d. une corrélation entre les differents indices mentionnés. Nous pouvons affirmer que les 'ciseaux des prix' étaient bien présents, contrairement à ce qui a été écrit (Genicot, Sosson). Le 'two-phase movement' Malthusien se produisait, tant pour le mouvement séculaire, que pour les mouvements demi-longs (les 'Kondratieffs' de 30 à 60 années). Le premier fléau de la Peste Noire (1349), se situe dans une période intermédiaire assez propice, ce qui peut aider à nous expliquer pourquoi ce fléau n'a pas provoqué une chute catastrophique de la population en Flandre. Les phases B de demi-long terme ont toujours duré plus longtemps que les phases A. Néanmoins la balance pour la conjoncture de l'économie rurale flamande est relativement positive, ce qui veut dire que nous avons pris une position intermédiaire entre les 'optimistes' et les 'pessimistes'. La longue durée de la crise est frappante : commencé vers ± 1300, elle a duré jusqu'à la fin du XVe siècle. Dès ± 1440/1450 une dernière phase B s'est produite, au moment où 'le beau seizième siècle' avait déjà démarré dans beaucoup de régions. La Flandre a donc suivi le 'modèle Bourguignon' (G. Sivery).

LES TRAITS PRINCIPAUX DES STRUCTURES DE LA SOCIETE RURALE FLAMANDE

Une interprétation fondamentale de la conjoncture ne peut se faire que par un examen profond de l'organisation de la production. Ici nous ne pouvons citer que quelques traits généraux.

I. Les possibilités techniques de l'agriculture

Durant la dernière phase de la croissance avant le commencement de la crise, notamment probablement entre ± 1230 et ± 1300, s'est développée en Flandre une technique agraire du type 'moderne', c'est-à-dire avec de très hauts rendements. Nous avons donc pu confirmer les thèses de Derville et Verhulst (1984) à ce sujet, et nous avons pu démontrer que ces techniques n'étaient pas seulement appliquées dans la région de la frontière Franco-Belge, mais qu'à l'intérieur de la Flandre on utilisait des techniques peut-être encore plus avancées. Dans les exploitations petites et moyennes des rendements de ± 1700 l. à l'hectare étaient chose commune et cela même sans qu'on y respectait la rotation triennale! Tout cela est devenu possible grâce à un haut niveau d'investissements par les paysans eux-mêmes (et aussi à cause des moyens qu'ils avaient pour introduire la stabulation). Autre caractéristique est la grande flexibilité de l'agriculture dû au fait que les coutûmes ('Flurzwang' etc.) qui existaient pourtant n'ont pas eu d'influence frénatrice vis-à-vis de l'agriculture. Le volume de la production était moins règlé par l'étendue de la surface cultivée (il n'y a eu peu ou pas de 'Wüstungen'), que par l'intensivité de la culture des champs, surtout en réduisant ou en augmentant le nombre des années de jachère ou de prairie artificielle temporaire ('trieu').

II. Le rôle de la circulation monétaire pour l'organisation et le financement de la production

Le degré élevé d'urbanisation a contribué à une circulation monétaire intensive à la campagne. Cela a provoqué qu'un pourcentage élevé des cens, rentes, baux etc. soit stipulé en espèces (plus de 'Geldrenten' que de 'Naturalrenten', répercussions, voir IV). Mais, cette économie 'monétaire' n'a pas stimulé les seigneurs à investir de manière directe dans l'agriculture. Donc, contrairement à certaines hypothèses, ici aussi pas de 'rent-investments', même pas par la bourgeoisie des villes (comp. Hilton (1962) après confirmé par Postan et Fourquin). Néanmoins les bourgeois riches des villes ont indirectement stimulé les investissements des paysans en procurant des fonds par moyen de ventes de rentes constituées.

III. L'étendue des exploitations en relation avec leur rentabilité

Dès la fin du XIIIe siècle, le réseau des exploitations rurales retrace l'image d'une large polarisation : une majorité de très petites exploitations de moins d'un hectare jusqu'a 4 ha. qui cultivaient moins que la moitié de la surface agricole. Les exploitations moyennes étaient peu présentes. Quoique les sources sont rares, il est probable que le nombre des paysans cultivants 4 à 10 ha. – l'exploitation qui est en Flandre le plus proche de l'exploitation de 'subsistance' – s'est accru au XIVe et XVe siècles, mais dans une mesure beaucoup moins prononcée qu'ailleurs (comp. Bois 1976, Hilton 1982). Cette évolution n'a pas stimulé l'économie comme on s'est figuré. (Bois, id., p. 352). Ces 'exploitations à une charrue' souffrent d'une part de faiblesses techniques (à juste titre déjà remarqué par M. Aymard 1981) et d'autre part de faiblesses structurelles parce qu'elles sont assez lourdement chargées à cause du fait qu'elles n'ont pu se développer qu'à cause de la naissance des baux de parcelles. Cela nous fait supposer que l'augmentation du nombre des 'laboureurs' a contribué à une baisse de la production.

IV. Les relations entre seigneurs et paysans, et l'organisation du prélèvement des seigneurs

1. Dans notre opinion une caractéristique fondamentale de la féodalité du XIe au XIIIe siècles n'est pas le prélèvement arbitraire (comme on l'a souvent écrit), mais le prélèvement fixe, ce qui a stimulé les seigneurs à encourager les paysans de faire des défrichements, puisque ces prélèvements ont subi de plus en plus de dépréciations dues à l'augmentation des prix ('the falling rate of feudal levy', voir Brenner 1976). De plus en plus les seigneurs ont réagi contre cette évolution, surtout quand les défrichements ont pris fin vers la fin du XIIIe siècle. Dès cette periode ils ont dû changer la structure du prélèvement en remplacant le plus possible les prélèvements fixes par des *prélèvements arbitraires* pour restaurer leurs revenus (voir ci-dessus 4).

2. Cette évolution a entrainé une *hausse du niveau de prélèvement* au bas Moyen Age (angl. : 'surplus extraction'; ce terme est interprété dans son sens le plus large et désigne tous les efforts de travail paysan qui sont dévolus aux seigneurs, donc aussi des destructions de guerre etc.). Il y a d'ailleurs également une nette corrélation entre le début des B-phases de demi-long terme et la hausse du ni-

veau de prélèvement. Dans ces types de cycles il n'y a pas de différence entre le taux du prélèvement et le niveau du prélèvement, comme Bois l'a constaté pour la Normandie. En Flandre les seigneurs ont seulement temporairement dû faire des concessions aux paysans quand les B-phases ont entrainé une baisse trop importante de la production.

3. La réaction seigneuriale se produisait *après une crise des finances* des institutions et des seigneurs. (Voir par exemple les difficultés de la grande abbaye bénédictine Saint-Pierre à Gand vers 1281).

4. *Les transformations de la seigneurie foncière.* Quelques transformations me semblent fondamentales :
- Dès ± 1270 l'offensif des bourgeois à la campagne est manifeste. Ils achètent des parcelles de terre et des fiefs, souvent pour en faire des 'fermes isolées' (M. Bloch).
- Les baux de parcelles remplacent de plus en plus les censives dès ± la même période (par divisions des 'réserves' anciennes, par transformation des 'tenures révocables', par l'affermage des censives etc.).
- L'affermage en général est en progression.

5. Sur le plan de *la seigneurie banale,* on peut faire deux remarques :
- Une réaction seigneuriale des seigneurs locaux n'est pas à exclure *a priori,* mais ne pouvait plus se produire, le pouvoir banal de ces personnes étant réduit d'une façon irréversible à cause d'une politique stratégique inventive des comtes de Flandre au plein Moyen Age.
- C'est l'état, le comte et puis le duc, qui a usurpé en une large mesure le pouvoir de la seigneurie banale et qui en a profité pour introduire des prélèvements assez arbitraires perçus régulièrement (les 'aides', puis aussi les amendes et les taxes de guerre) pour établir un 'féodalisme d'état' en pleine expansion.

6. *Les limites aux transformations structurelles du prélèvement.*
On n'a p.ex. pas pu introduire en Flandre, comme en Italie du Nord le métayage sur une grande échelle. La réaction féodale sur le niveau de la seigneurie foncière avait ses limites. De même pour la

seigneurie banale. Nous avons pu calculer que depuis la fin du XIVe siècle jusqu'en ± 1460 les impôts directs dépassaient rarement 5 % de la valeur annuelle de la récolte (le plus souvent pas plus que 2 à 3 %). Après cette date cela a augmenté vers 10 à 15 %, mais comparé au Brabant, à la Hollande, le Hainaut et le Namurois, les flamands continuaient probablement à payer par habitant beaucoup moins. Au milieu du XIVe siècle les exigences du fisc étaient 4 fois plus importantes en Normandie que vers 1480 en Flandre. Qu'est-ce qui a causé ces entraves?

L'idée élaborée par Brenner sur le rôle de la relation entre les sujets du prélèvement ('the surplus extraction relations') dans un contexte different nous semble ici applicable et même fondamental. C'est la concurrence entre les classes dirigeantes de la société (l'état, les seigneurs, la bourgeoisie et le clergé) qui a contribué à déterminer le niveau du prélèvement (Brenner 1976 et 1982). En ce qui concerne la situation dès la fin du XIIIe siècle, on a déjà noté le 'knock-out' de la noblesse, mais c'était surtout de la lutte entre les grandes villes et le pouvoir central que la Flandre a pu profiter (malgré les guerres civiles entre les deux pouvoirs). C'étaient les villes qui avaient le pouvoir dans la représentation des Etats et c'étaient eux qui ont réussi à limiter les exigences du fisc. D'autre part le comte a toujours essayé de limiter la vente des terres à la campagne aux bourgeois. C'est aussi à cause de la lutte entre villes, seigneurs et le comte que l'institution de la bourgeoisie foraine a pu se développer dès le début du XIIIe siècle, ce qui a donné aux paysans aisés la possibilité de s'opposer contre toutes formes d'exploitation illégale. Pour finir, on peut ajouter que le fait que, dès le XIIe siècle déjà, le pouvoir de la seigneurie foncière et de la seigneurie banale se trouvait de plus en plus entre les mains de seigneurs différents, a rendu des changements radicaux des structures de la seigneurie foncière difficile.

QUELQUES CONCLUSIONS EXPLICATIVES

Il est impossible de résumer en quelques pages le modèle explicatif que nous avons établi. Nous nous limitons aux remarques suivantes.

1. Comme Boserup, Brenner, Bois et autres nous rejetons le modèle néo-Malthusianiste qui fait de la démographie le *primum movens* de la société. Ce modèle néglige non seulement les structures de la société, mais il ne peut pas expliquer la diversité régionale de l'intensité de la crise (Brenner 1982, p. 23). Selon leur raisonnement d'ailleurs la crise aurait dû toucher la Flandre d'une manière extrêmement grave, puisque la tension entre démographie et production n'était nulle part ailleurs si grande. Le contraire s'est produit.

2. La crise doit être vue en rapport avec les structures de la production qui se sont instaurées avant le XIVe siècle. Elle est le résultat de la baisse de la productivité du travail qui s'est produite à cause des prélèvements féodaux et le manque d'investissements des seigneurs à la campagne qui ont épongé une large partie du produit agricole (cfr. les études de Hilton, Brenner, Bois et Kosminsky). La crise est aussi en rapport direct avec une hausse du volume de prélèvement qui doit être vue dans le contexte de la crise des finances des grands propriétaires fonciers et des seigneurs à la fin du XIIIe siècle et des transformations des relations entre les classes au pouvoir comme on l'a résumé.

3. Ce sont ces mêmes facteurs qui sont decisifs pour expliquer la légèreté relative de la crise en Flandre. Comme nous l'avons décrit, les paysans flamands ont pu réagir partiellement contre la baisse de la productivité au XIIIe siècle grâce au fait que des nouvelles techniques agricoles ont pu se généraliser. Cela fut à son tour possible par le fait que les paysans eux-mêmes avaient assez de moyens pour faire des investissements 'de profondeur' dans cette région urbanisée. Ce n'est néanmoins pas le facteur géographique (comme l'a écrit e.a. Irsigler) qui explique à lui seul ces investissements. De nouveau il faut introduire les structures économiques dans l'explication. Nous sommes d'avis que les paysans flamands ont pu profiter plus qu'ailleurs de la hausse des prix agricoles et de la relative stabilité des rentes et des prélèvements avant le XIVe siècle. Le fait que beaucoup de rentes et de cens étaient stipulés en argent joue un rôle important (dévaluation plus rapide de leur valeur). En outre, à cause de la concentration des marchés urbains en Flandre la terre cultivée y a une plusvalue. Puisqu'il est probable que pendant les phases de hausse la demande des produits agricoles augmentait, cette valeur ajoutée a augmenté plus dans des régions urbanisées

que dans des régions moins urbanisées (où le commerce intermédiaire était plus important etc.). En Flandre les paysans eux-mêmes ont pu profiter plus largement de cette hausse de valeur ajoutée à cause du 'falling rate of feudal levy'. C'est aussi pour cette raison qu'en Flandre les paysans étaient poussés à l'investissement, tant plus parce que la bourgeoisie était prête à investir des fonds de manière indirecte, notamment par la vente de rentes constituées!

Malgré l'importance que nous avons attribuée aux techniques agricoles pour l'explication de la légèreté relative de la crise, l'anticipation de la plupart des 'inventions' vers le XIIIe siècle a pour conséquence logique que la théorie de Slicher van Bath (1960), que la crise elle-même a poussé les paysans flamands à la recherche de nouvelles techniques, doit être rejetée.

Puisque s'est une réaction féodale qui a enfin neutralisé partiellement la riposte des paysans flamands à la baisse de la productivité, se sont des 'freins' structuraux qui étaient responsables pour le soulagement des effects de la crise. Mais ces entraves ont été mentionnées plus haut.

REFERENCES

E. Aerts et E. Van Cauwenberghe, 'Die Grafschaft Flandern und die sogenannte spätmittelalterliche Depression', F. Seibt, W. Eberhard, éd., *Europa 1400. Die Krise des Spätmittelalters* (Stuttgart, 1984), 95-116.

M. Aymard, 'L'Europe Moderne : féodalité ou féodalités', *Annales E.S.C.*, 3 (1981), 426-434.

G. Bois, *Crise du féodalisme. Economie rurale et démographie en Normandie orientale du début du 14e siècle au milieu du 16e siècle* (Paris, 1976).

R. Brenner, 'Agrarian Class Structure and Economic Development in Pre-Industrial Europe', *Past and Present,* 70 (févr. 1976), 30-75.

R. Brenner, 'The Agrarian Roots of European Capitalism', *Past and Present,* 97 (nov. 1982), 16-113.

R. Hilton, 'Rent and capital formation in feudal society', *Deuxième conférence d'histoire économique. Aix-en-Provence,* tôme II (Paris/La Haye, 1962), 33-68.

R. Hilton, 'A Crisis of Feudalism', *Past and Present,* 97 (nov. 1982), 3-19.

B.H. Slicher van Bath, 'The Rise of Intensive Husbandry in the Low Countries', *Britain and the Netherlands. Papers delivered to the Oxford-Netherlands Historical Conference* (Londres, 1960), 130-153.

E. Thoen, *Landbouwekonomie en bevolking in Vlaanderen gedurende de late Middeleeuwen en het begin van de Moderne Tijden. Testregio : de kasselrijen van Oudenaarde en Aalst* (Centre Belge d'Histoire Rurale 90) (2 tômes, Gand, 1988) (traduction prévu en anglais).

H. Van der Wee, 'Crisistypologie en structuurwijzigingen in de Nederlanden (15e-16e eeuw)', Id., éd., *Historische aspecten van de economische groei* (Anvers/Utrecht, 1971), 100-127.

R. Van Uytven, 'La Flandre et le Brabant "terres de promission" sous les ducs de Bourgogne?', *Revue du Nord,* 93 (1961), 281-317.

A. Verhulst, 'L'économie rurale de la Flandre et la dépression économique du bas Moyen Age', *Etudes Rurales,* 10 (1963), 63-80.

A. Verhulst, 'L'intensification et la commercialisation de l'agriculture dans les Pays-Bas méridionaux au XIIIe siècle', *Mélanges offerts à Jean-Jacques Hoebanx* (Bruxelles, 1984), 89-100.

EARLY MODERN PERIOD

RURAL CHANGE IN THE DUTCH PROVINCE OF DRENTHE, 1600-1910

JAN BIELEMAN

During the Republic (c. 1600-1795) the state of Drenthe extended as far as the modern province, an area of about 266,000 ha. It was a rather isolated region, surrounded by vast blanket bogs and consisting mainly of a boulder clay plateau, which had been partly eroded by melting streams and then covered with an infertile layer of sand. In the early 17th century the *Landschap* must have been an almost empty steppe of heath and blanket bogs over which small villages and hamlets of the *esdorpen* type with their *essen* or open fields were scattered like islands in an ocean. In 1630 Drenthe had about 22,000 inhabitants, which means a density of no more than 7 to 8 people per km^2.

Farming here, almost four centuries ago, cannot be understood unless it is constantly remembered that farming life then was pervaded with so many more hazards than it is today.

Coupled to this, the circumstances of a distant market and a very infertile environment constrained farmers to manage their farm on a very extensive basis. Extensiveness was also dictated by their endeavours to minimize all the risks they had to cope with. In fact risk-minimizing was one of the main principles that ruled farming in those days. It urged farmers to run a very diversified type of farming.

As a result, during the 17th century farms were large and possessed a remarkable number of cattle and horses. Although these farms varied in area, about 8.6 ha of arable land was fairly common.

As in the other parts of the sandy regions of the Netherlands and on the North German *'Geest',* these farms had a rather high complement of horses. A so-called *'vol bedrijf'* (a farm unit with full rights) with four adult horses was widespread. The function of the horse however meant more than just the supply of draught power on the farm. Especially on the four-horse farms, horse breeding was an important source of income.

Another important feature on this large type of farm was the great number of cattle. An early 17th century notice contains the information that on a *'vol bedrijf'* with 8.6 ha arable land, 24 cows (including the young cattle) were kept. Cattle breeding in the open-field villages of central and eastern Drenthe at that time however had a completely different character than it had later on. Cattle breeding then and there was fitted in a Von Thünen zonation which had been laid out over northwestern Europe since the 16th century and in which Dutch and Flemish towns were the focus. In this way Drenthe played a part in a interregional labour division in meat production. It was therefore that the large number of cattle on the *esdorpen* farms included a relatively large number of young bullocks, pastured on the extensive poor commons. After some years these bullocks were driven to the much better pastures in Holland or other coastal provinces where they were grazed for one more season. They were then sold for slaughter in the towns.

With the rise of the textile industry in the second half of the 16th century, the number of sheep must have increased on an important scale. However small the production of wool by a single Drenthian heather sheep might have been – seen through modern eyes – this part of farming at that time was also an important source of income.

Notwithstanding the important place of livestock, arable farming was still the pivot on which all the activities on these farms turned. But the arable land on the *essen* was used in a rather extensive way. Not all arable land there was actually ploughed, and the marginal fringes of the open fields were in use as 'outfield'. A part of this outfield usually lay fallow. Once in a while a farmer would grow one or two crops of rye or buckwheat without using manure and labour. One of the most important advantages of this system was the accumulation of humus as plant nutrients, leading to an improvement in the physical structure of the soil of these marginal parts of the field.

The field system enabled the community to use the open fields for pasturing after the crop had been harvested. In fact the open field was open for grazing a greater part of the year, except for the growing season of the corn crop in spring and summer. To enable the farming community to make use of the open fields in this way, each farmer was bound by a set of regulations. Rules for grazing based on these regulations meant that the right of the individual farmer were, to a great extent, secondary to the rights of the whole community. This can be conceived as a typical aspect of the extensiveness of farming here this time. This practice of pasturing on the stubble contributed considerably to the maintenance of the soil fertility of the *essen.* Therefore it was probably sufficient for the farmer to manure only those parts of the field which were to be sown with winter rye.

The consequence however of this extensive treatment of the arable land was very low yields. During the 17th century the seed-yield ratios must have been no higher than 1 to 3 or 4.

Farming in Drenthe during the first half of the 17th century was dominated by an expanding economy. The growth of the number of cattle and sheep was a clear symptom of that. However just after 1660 there was a reversal of the upward movement of the economy which had dominated the previous decades. The direct causes were essentially twofold. Except for some short periods of recovery, the prices of agricultural products continued to decline until about 1730. What is more, at the same time farmers had to battle against a severe increase in costs, caused by a string of new and heavier taxes. This tax burden culminated around the end of the 17th and the first two decades of the 18th century. Farmers then were sandwiched between falling prices and rising costs. Without doubt the years 1690-1720 were the tragic nadir in this movement. The actual burden of taxation (expressed in an equivalent quantity of rye) just after 1700 was at least four times as high as it had been just before 1650.

The only way open for farmers to withstand this scissor-like movement of prices and costs, was to try to raise their production. Given the overall conditions on the *esdorpen,* this was only possible by intensifying their farming system. The only thing for them left to do was to work harder or longer themselves or to make more use of cheap hired labour. At the same time they could dispose of all kinds of strictly non-agricultural activities that had been traditionally done within the household itself. These activities were now left to a group of specialists – artisans and shopkeepers. In so doing, a basis of existence was created for a group that beforehand formed only a small part of the rural community. The need for hired labour was at the same time a basis of existence for a group of small farmers or cottagers (*keuters*) who, as farm labourers, formed a permanent potential labour force which could be used by the farmers whenever needed. In a period when agriculture suffered from heavy taxation and low prices these two social groups underwent a rather substantial growth.

To cope with their situation farmers tried to put more rye on the market than they had been used to do. For this purpose they took the outfield parts of the *essen* into more permanent use. The buckwheat that they started to grow there more permanently, came to be used to meet household consumption needs. Later on potatoes gave a still better possibility to do so, and this is probably why the larger farmers were the innovators of potato-cultivation in Drenthe.

The expansion of the area under crop and the intensification of using the outfield more permanently was only made possible by the use of more manure and by spending more effort in preparing it. The infield was also probably more heavily manured than before. There were strong indications that after the beginning of the 18th century the techniques used to maintain the fertility of the open fields were fundamentally changed. Under the traditional system of sod manuring (*plaggenbemesting*), dung in the stable was absorbed by humus (sods or *plaggen*) cut from the waste lands and then taken to the field. From the early 18th the quantity of these sods used in this way increased substantially. By doing so farmers brought more humus (and so plant nutrients) to their arable land. At the same time the common grazing of the open fields was more strongly regulated and forced back.

The process of intensification found expression in a decrease of the numbers of horses and cattle. During the 17th century conditions for extensive cattle breeding became less favourable because of a decrease in meat consumption in the towns. After about 1690, farmers began to reduce the number of cattle in favour of sheep. As a consequence of this proces of contraction by the beginning of the 19th century it was rare to find as many as 24 cows on a farm.

The keeping of sheep, which had been reduced because of a decline in the textile industry in the third quarter of the 17th century, began to expand again after the end of the same century. Moreover, losses from liver fluke decreased throughout the 18th century. This was a result of draining the wet parts of the commons, so that they were more suitable for the grazing of sheep.

A more constant number of sheep meant better management of the whole farm.

Since the 1690's, but especially after the second period of the cattle plague, cattle was more or less substituted more and more by sheep in their role of producers of manure.

The outcome of this process of intensification of the farming system in the *esdorpen* was an important increase in yield. By many coherent measures, farmers succeeded in breaking through the medieval ceiling of productivity by almost doubling the seed-yield ratio. In fact the benefits were even more important because they could sell a relatively larger part of this doubled yield.

At the turn of the 18th century into the 19th century there was a sudden and fundamental change in the pattern of population growth. After 1800 within a period of less than one century the population of Drenthe quadrupled.

At first the rapid population growth led to an increase of a landless proletariat that lived more or less in the margins of agriculture. However, at the same time, some changes in agriculture were foreshadowed. They soon were to lead to a completely new orientation of the farming system, in which – again – cattle was getting an important role. This time together with pig breeding and fattening.

The relative development of grain prices on the one hand and the price of butter on the other was caused by the demand for meat and dairy products from the early industrializing countries like Britain over against the flooding of the European grain markets with cheap corn coming from the south of Russia. Soon after that, the breaking down of toll barriers by the countries around the Netherlands in the 1840's caused a strong suction on the Dutch markets. The free trade which was now possible, effected a true revolution in prices.

Over a period of one and a half centuries livestock in the *esdorpen* region had been structurally reduced. However, as a result of these developments, it had been increasing since the 1840's. In a relatively short period of time the number of horses, cattle increased again. New breeds of pigs were now introduced to meet new demands. The development of the relative prices of grain on one hand and of livestock and livestock products on the other, caused a transition in the farming system. Products from the arable land were no longer sold on the market, but kept on the farm to be fed to the animals. Former cash crops now became fodder crops. In addition farmers also began to feed more oilcake to their cattle than they had before, which also stimulated milk yield.

Over the next decades, this transition in farming was completed. The rye-producing farm of former days had become an improving type of farm (*'étage-bedrijf'*), selling improved products like butter and pigs (pork). This process began in the southwestern part of the province, but before the beginning of the great agricultural depression (1878-1895) it had reached its completion. This new improved type of farming system was based on a much higher labour intensity. This meant also that now it became possible to build up a living on a much smaller type of farm than before. Ever since the 1840's, in a relatively short period of time a group of one-horse-farms came into existence. However at the end of the seventies all kinds of protective measures were taken by the importing countries surrounding the Netherlands – whether or not disguised – which, in the mid-1890's finally led to the closing of their frontiers for cattle and pigs. At the same time however, the export of freshly slaughtered pigs had been multiplied and soon the Dutch sandy regions supplied the majority of the British pork market. This new form of pig feeding appeared to be decisive, especially for the group of small and very small farmers, because the pigs could be brought to the desired weight in a short time and the money invested could be realized more quickly. Thus the favourable situation of farming on the Dutch sandy regions in relation to its market in strongly industrialized Britain created a rather special set-up. The completion of the railway system at the right moment channelled a particular demand which was well suited to the social structure of the rural population and farming in this region at that time.

However pig breeding as a part of farming would not have become so important if at the same time the production and sales of farm butter had not been organized in a different way and on a different scale. On the British market (the most important sales market for Dutch butter), ruthless competition and sinking prices were a consequence of the increasing supply of butter. The export of Dutch farm butter was threatened. Because of the existing sales channels through which farmers exchanged their butter with local tradesmen or shopkeepers for oilcake and other materials, they initially had no answer to the crumbling of their market position.

The only thing left to them was to try to organize the processing of butter and its sales on a larger scale and on a cooperative basis, which, it was hoped, would eventually lead to a better product. The first steam-powered creamery was established in the southwest of the province in 1889 and was soon followed by others. A real breakthrough was the introduction of a cheap, small-scale, hand-powered factory (*handkracht-fabriek*).

This new type of large-scale processing consolidated and improved the market position of the established farmer. The creameries also enabled very small farmers and land labourers to render commercially viable the small quantities of milk they could produce with one or two dairy cows. With the skimmed milk or buttermilk they got back from the creamery, they now could feed a few 'London pigs' every year. This group which had previously broken away from the traditional group of larger farmers, was now able to build up a more independent position. On the basis of this further development in an intensified and improving type of farming and stimulated by a growing economy, the turn of the 20th century saw a completely new category of very small farms come into existence, besides the already increased group of one-horse farms. Notwithstanding the growth of the cattle population since the 1840's, due to the increase of the number of small and very small farmers, the average keeper of cattle in the central parts of the province in 1910 had only about 7 to 8 cows (including the young cattle).

In the early 20th century the rural community of this sandy region was defined by a large group of small and very small farmers. The group of traditional *'volle bedrijven'* which in the 17th century had formed the body of rural society, then formed only a small minority. Initially everybody had confidence in this development which in fact was based on a market beyond the national border, with all the risks this involved. The actual vulnerability of these small and very small family holdings came to light soon afterwards, in the 1920's and 1930's.

REFERENCE

For bibliography and further details see my *Boeren op het Drentse zand 1600-1910. Een nieuwe visie op de 'oude' landbouw.* (Afdeling Agrarische Geschiedenis Landbouwuniversiteit Wageningen. A.A.G. Bijdragen, 29) (Wageningen, 1987). With English summary.

POPULATION, PRICES, AND WEATHER IN PREINDUSTRIAL EUROPE

PATRICK RICHARD GALLOWAY

There were few phenomena of more interest to preindustrial Europeans than the harvest, the weather, marriage, reproduction, and death. The present study focuses on the interaction of these variables from one year to the next using a methodology that adds a dynamic dimension to the usual cross-sectional analysis. The significance, temporal structure, and magnitude of the impact of fluctuations in grain prices and seasonal temperature on variations in nuptiality, fertility, and mortality are examined among the rural and urban, the young and old, and the rich and poor of preindustrial Europe.

Chapter 2 begins with an analysis of the patterns of responses of vital rates to variations in grain prices in a number of preindustrial European countries. The importance of annual variations in grain prices to annual changes in the standard of living is discussed. Inferences are made about the relative strenghts of the short-term Malthusian preventive and positive checks and the role development, income, and urbanization levels may play in the determination of the timing and magnitude of these checks.

The impact of variations in weather on fluctuations in pıices, fertility, and mortality is examined in Chapter 3. The effects of changes in prices, and winter, spring, summer, autumn, and annual temperatures on variations in fertility and mortality are estimated and comparisons made across countries.

The next few chapters focus on age-specific demographic responses to fluctuations in prices and temperature in an attempt to shed some light on the underlying processes that may be determining the responses observed in the preceding chapters. Sweden is unique in the quantity and quality of its published historical age-specific annual demographic events and its data are used throughout. Chapter 4 explores the impact of variations in prices on changes in age-specific nuptiality rates in Sweden. This is followed in Chapter 5 by an examination of the roles prices and seasonal temperature may play in changes in Swedish age-specific fertility rates. Problems centering around the complicated interaction of behavioural and biological fertility responses are discussed. Chapter 6 is an analysis of the impact of prices and temperature variations on fluctuations in age-specific mortality in Sweden, one of the more rural countries in Europe, and in London, the largest metropolis in Europe at the time.

A detailed analysis of the impact of changes in prices and temperature on variations in deaths by cause in Sweden and Londen is undertaken in Chapter 7. Fluctuations in deaths from typhus, smallpox, dysentery, tuberculosis, and other causes along with changes in the maternal mortality rate, stillbirth rate, and infant mortality rate are examined within the context of variations in prices and temperature.

The next two chapters explore the impact of price changes on fluctuations in demographic events among the rich and poor in two distinct socioeconomic settings. Chapter 8 analyzes these relationships among nineteen rural administrative districts in Arhus Diocese in Denmark, while Chapter 9 examines eight parish groups in the large city of Rouen in France.

Chapter 10 compares and contrasts the impact of changes in prices on variations in vital events among the rich and poor in European countries, Arhus rural administrative districts, and parish groups in Rouen using pooled data.

Chapter 11 takes a different tack away from short-term analysis to an examination of long-term fluctuations in climate and population in the preindustrial era.

Each chapter was written so that it may be read independently, once the basic methodology (described in Chapter 2) is understood. As a consequence, replication of the discussion of some previous research and theory was necessary. Those interested primarily in the impact of short-term seasonal temperature changes on variations in vital rates need only read Chapters 2, 3, 5, 6 and 7. The reader who is mainly interested in short-term differential responses of vital rates to fluctuations in grain prices among the rich and poor need only read Chapters 2, 8, 9 and 10. Long-term fluctuations in climate and population are discussed in detail only in Chapter 11.

Finally, the same statistical method, described in Chapter 2, is employed throughout in order to facilitate comparative discussion. The graphic displays of the statistical results are presented in such a manner that comparisons can be made not only within a chapter but among chapters. With a few exceptions noted in the text and tables, the calendar year (January 1 to December 31) is used throughout. In the regressions, calendar year prices are only used in association with calendar year vital rates, and harvest year prices are only used in conjunction with harvest year vital rates. Within a chapter, the text is presented first followed by tables and then figures. The great mass of detailed statistical results may be found in the Appendix Tables.

Analysis of the responses of annual variations in vital rates to annual fluctuations in grain prices in nine preindustrial European countries confirms the existence of short-term Malthusian preventive and positive checks. The structure and magnitude of the preventive check is similar across all countries and time periods. On the other hand, the strength of the positive check varies widely and in accord with measures of economic development. The magnitude of the positive check relative to the preventive check diminishes as economic development increases. Among the countries examined, wide variations in population growth rate in response to price changes can be attributed primarily to differences in the strength of the positive check.

Among the nine European countries examined, significant increases in mortality and decreases in fertility are associated with cold winters and warm summers. The strongest effects are generally found in poorer countries.

In Sweden, first marriages and remarriages decrease significantly with elevated prices. Nuptiality increases as a result of heightened adult mortality, with remarriages displaying the greatest sensitivity.

Fertility declines significantly one year after an increase in prices in Sweden. The magnitude of this decline is about the same across all age groups. Cold winters, cold springs, and warm summers are associated with decreased fertility, with the strongest responses generally found among other married women.

Age-specific mortality responses to price increases in both Sweden and London take the form of a U-shaped curve, with mortality among the younger and older age groups being most affected at lag 0. Cold winters and warm summers are associated with increased mortality in all age groups, with the young in

Sweden and the elderly in London showing the greatest sensitivity.

Typhus deaths increase dramatically in both Sweden and London in association with elevated prices. High prices are also associated with heightened mortality from dysentery, whooping cough, tuberculosis, infant mortality, and stillbirths in Sweden and fever and smallpox in London. In general epidemic mortality seems to be associated with high prices in Sweden and London, although smallpox in Sweden is not affected by price changes.

Cold winters and hot summers are associated with significant increases in deaths from many causes. Cold winters tend to increase typhus, tuberculosis, and infant mortality in Sweden. Hot summers seem to be associated with a dramatic increase in dysentery and typhus deaths in Sweden, along with smaller, yet significant, increases in tuberculosis and infant mortality. In London, cold winters and hot summers are associated with significant increases in the number of deaths from fever, consumption, infancy, old age, apoplexy, dropsy, and diarrhea.

An examination of the annual responses of vital events to variations in grain prices among rural districts in Arhus Diocese in Denmark in the eighteenth century reveals that as a result of elevated grain prices the fertility of the rural poor decreases and the mortality of the rural poor increases significantly. Variations in fertility and mortality among the rural rich are less affected by changes in grain prices.

A similar analysis of groups of parishes in the city of Rouen from 1681 tot 1787 reveals significant differences between rich and poor parishes in the strength of the preventive check. The urban poor respond to a price increase by dramatically decreasing fertility, while the fertility of the urban rich is virtually unaffected. An increase in prices is associated with relatively large increases in mortality, suggesting a strong positive check. However, little difference can be found between the rich and poor areas in the magnitude or timing of mortality responses to price variations.

Finally, an analysis of population, meteorological, and agricultural series over the long run in Europe, China, and North America suggests that an important driving force behind long-term fluctuations in population may be long-term variations in climate and their effects on carrying capacity and vital rates.

LA FAMILLE ET LA SOCIETE DANS LES QUARTIERS SUD DE VARSOVIE AU XVIIIe SIECLE STRUCTURES DEMOGRAPHIQUES

Cezary Kuklo

Depuis une vingtaine d'années, l'historiographie mondiale a connu un développement très dynamique dans le domaine des recherches sur l'histoire économique de la famille ancienne. Cela s'explique aisément : la plupart des modes d'organisation de la vie économique – tant à la campagne que dans la ville à l'époque préindustrielle – étaient fondés sur la famille. Il est regrettable que l'historiographie polonaise ne possède pas encore de vastes études consacrées aux structures internes des familles de la Pologne ancienne.

Le travail présenté vise principalement à étudier, à partir du mouvement naturel de la population, les circonstances qui contribuent à la formation et à la désintégration de la famille ainsi que les dimensions et les structures de celle-ci. Le cadre géographique est celui de Varsovie qui était la plus grande agglomération polonaise de la période préindustrielle. L'auteur estime que les analyses démographiques constituent une base fondamentale pour les recherches concernant l'histoire économique de la famille. La dimension de la famille et sa structure interne ont déterminé la plupart des choix et des activités économiques. Par ailleurs, le potentiel biologique d'une famille résulte de processus sociaux et économiques bien définis.

L'objet de notre étude était d'établir les paramètres de base – restés inconnus jusqu'à présent – des caractéristiques de la famille urbaine de l'ancienne Pologne, tels que l'âge de mariage, la natalité dans les familles, la fréquence des mariages et des remariages, le taux de fécondité (naissances légitimes et illégitimes), la mortalité selon l'âge et le sexe. Une attention particulière a été réservée à l'influence de la situation économique de la ville préindustrielle sur les phénomènes démographiques. A cet égard, il importait de déterminer si une conjoncture économique favorable ou difficile avait stimulé ou au contraire freiné d'une façon ou d'une autre le potentiel de la population étudiée.

La présente étude avait également pour objet d'appliquer pour la première fois sur une aussi vaste échelle la technique du calcul électronique qui est encore, en Pologne, d'un emploi très limité dans les recherches historiques. Le travail avec ordinateur, méthode peu répandue parmi les historiens polonais, n'a pas été sans problèmes.

La reconstitution des familles concerne des ménages qui ont contracté mariage dans la paroisse Sainte-Croix à Varsovie, qui y ont habité de 1740 à 1799 et qui avaient terminé le processus de génération avant le début du XIXe siècle. Afin d'établir le rapport entre la démographie et les changements sociaux et économiques à Varsovie et afin de comparer notre étude à celles effectuées à l'étranger, il a été décidé de diviser le matériel recueilli en deux groupes, le premier concernant la période 1740-1769 et le second la période 1770-1799.

Sur base de l'analyse de plus de 80.000 actes de naissance, de mariage et de décès, 1.501 familles 'fermées' (dont les dates de mariage et de décès d'un des époux sont connues) et 404 familles 'ouvertes' (pour lesquelles on ne possède aucune donnée concernant le décès des époux) ont été reconstituées. En outre, pour 957 familles reconstituées, l'âge de la mère au moment du mariage a pu être établi, ce qui a permis de faire des analyses détaillées du nombre d'enfants dans la famille et de la fécondité des femmes.

L'auteur a reconstruit le mouvement saisonnier des mariages à Varsovie au XVIIIe siècle. Il se caractérise par l'existence de deux sommets très évidents : janvier-février et septembre-novembre, et d'un troisième moins manifeste, au mois de juillet. La comparaison avec d'autres modèles concernant des villes d'Europe occidentale dont le niveau d'industrialisation et le chiffre de la population étaient très différents, a mis en relief la prépondérance des facteurs économiques. Indépendamment de certaines différences existant dans le modèle saisonnier européen des mariages – par exemple entre catholiques et protestants –, on constate une influence des changements saisonniers du travail agricole. En confrontant le prix du froment et du seigle avec le salaire des journaliers non qualifiés, on a distingué les années de plus haute et de plus basse conjoncture économique pour l'ensemble du XVIIIe siècle. En établissant le rapport entre ces périodes et le nombre de mariages contractés à la même époque, on peut affirmer que, généralement, le mouvement des mariages dans la Varsovie préindustrielle se caractérisait par des fluctuations parallèles aux changements de la situation économique. Généralement les années de bons salaires coïncident directement (ou avec une année de retard) avec les sommets matrimoniaux. Alors que les périodes de grande prospérité ou de crise dans la ville préindustrielle ont remarquablement influencé les attitudes à l'égard du mariage, l'analyse du déroulement des grandes épidémies, par exemple de peste, démontre qu'en général la population renonçait alors à fonder une famille.

L'historiographie polonaise souligne avec une certaine prédilection l'originalité des structures économiques, sociales et politiques de la Pologne ancienne. Pourtant, dans nos études sur la famille urbaine des années 1740-1799, on retrouve un des traits les plus caractéristiques de la famille de l'Europe occidentale, à savoir l'âge de mariage assez élevé des hommes. A Varsovie, il était, lors du premier mariage, de 29 ans en moyenne. La longueur relative de la période nécessaire pour acquérir la stabilité matérielle explique ce délai. Toutefois, à l'opposé de la tendance en Europe occidentale, les jeunes filles de Varsovie contractaient leur mariage beaucoup plus tôt que les Françaises, les Allemandes ou les Anglaises. Dans les années 1740-1769, au moment du premier mariage, elles avaient en moyenne 23 ans (âge médian : 21,8) et au cours du dernier tiers du XVIIIe siècle, cet âge baisse encore d'un an. Par rapport à l'Europe occidentale, il en résulte une maternité plus précoce. La grande différence d'âge entre les époux au moment du mariage (6-7 ans) constitue un autre trait distinctif.

La mort prématurée d'un des époux – souvent celle de la femme à la suite d'un accouchement effectué dans de mauvaises conditions d'hygiène – a influencé la durée relativement brève du mariage; elle est de 15 ans en moyenne. Pendant les années sans catastrophes naturelles et sans crises économiques, les remariages ne constituent qu'un tiers de tous les mariages contractés. Leur nombre monte brusquement aprés des périodes de catastrophes ou de mortalité élevée; à ce moment, les remariages représentent 45-50 % du total. Le remariage était une nécessité économique et sociale car souvent la femme aidait son mari dans l'atelier ou l'entreprise commerciale, tout en assurant la garde des enfants. En outre, les règles des corporations interdisaient parfois aux veuves de diriger l'atelier après la mort de leur mari, ce qui les contraignait à rechercher un nouvel époux. Cependant l'enquête réalisée montre que les chances des veufs et des veuves n'étaient pas égales. Dans les familles reconstituées, près de la moitié des veufs ont contracté un nouveau mariage alors qu'un tiers des veuves ont fait de même. De plus les veufs se remariaient beaucoup plus rapidement.

Une grande partie des recherches a été consacrée au nombre d'enfants des familles varsoviennes. Cette question a été étudiée pour toutes les familles fermées reconstituées. L'étude montre qu'au cours des 60 dernières années du XVIIIe siècle le nombre moyen de naissances dans les mariages féconds a baissé. Les familles formées au cours des années 1740-1769 présentent une moyenne de 5,0 enfants tandis que cette moyenne descend à 3,8 enfants pour les trois décennies suivantes. On a observé le même phénomène dans les familles complètes où la femme mariée avait atteint l'âge de 45 ans. Durant la première période, ces couples ont eu en moyenne 7,1 enfants, durant la seconde 6,8.

En recherchant les causes et les conditions qui ont influencé le changement du taux annuel des naissances au XVIIIe siècle, l'auteur a remarqué des attitudes procréatrices pendant les catastrophes naturelles. Il a ainsi élaboré le modèle d'une famille varsovienne et il l'a confronté au modèle des relations matrimoniales de la Pologne rurale ancienne, ainsi qu'à celui des grandes villes européennes et de leur campagne. Il en résulte que, malgré les conditions de vie différentes dans la ville préindustrielle et à la campagne, il existe une ressemblance entre le modèle saisonnier de la vie d'une famille à la campagne et dans la ville : le printemps se caractérise par des réactions biologiques plus nombreuses, l'été par la diminution de leur nombre. Il faut néanmoins remarquer que dans les familles urbaines, elles se répartissent plus régulièrement entre tous les mois de l'année.

Les valeurs du coefficient de corrélation du nombre annuel de baptêmes et des prix moyens et annuels du seigle (r = 0,22) et du blé (r = 0,41) ne sont pas une preuve suffisante d'une association régulière entre les variations de fécondité et celles du prix des céréales. En revanche, le coefficient de corrélation du salaire journalier d'un ouvrier sans qualifications (r = 0,93) démontre l'influence des tendances économiques à long terme sur les différences des niveaux de fécondité.

On peut supposer qu'un niveau de vie croissant augmente la fécondité de la population urbaine préindustrielle. Les périodes de bons salaires réels dans l'économie de la Pologne ancienne signifient une baisse des prix des produits alimentaires et des conditions de vie plus favorables, même pour les plus pauvres.

Le coefficient de corrélation entre le nombre de décès et le prix de céréales (pour le seigle r = 0,22 et pour le blé 0,56) ne permet pas d'établir une correspondance entre l'augmentation du prix de la nourriture et une mortalité plus forte. On ne peut pas dire qu'une période de baisse des prix se caractérise par une diminution du nombre des décès. On peut, en revanche, être étonné par la coïncidence très visible de la courbe des décès avec celle des salaires à Varsovie (r = 0,74). Il est difficile d'admettre que les périodes de prospérité économique, avec des salaires très élevés, se caractérisent par unc mortalité plus élevée. On peut cependant tenter de l'expliquer.

La corrélation positive et élevée entre les décès et les salaires témoigne, selon l'auteur, d'une immigration de population. Le redressement économique (hausse des salaires, développement de la construction, essor du commerce et des entreprises industrielles) entraînait une concentration de la main-d'œuvre et un accroissement plus dynamique du nombre d'habitants de la capitale. On y observe alors un afflux de population dont ni les baptêmes ni les mariages ne se trouvent enregistrés dans les registres varsoviens. La majorité de cette population récemment installée à Varsovie y est décédée. Les salaires plus élevés observés durant de longues périodes et résultant du développement urbain augmentent globalement le nombre des décès. L'avenir montrera si cette explication peut être maintenue.

Le travail réalisé englobe aussi l'étude du phénomène des enfants illégitimes et des enfants trouvés dont le nombre était considérable dans la Varsovie préindustrielle du XVIIIe siècle. Dans les années dites normales – sans grandes catastrophes naturelles – les enfants illégitimes représentaient en moyenne 8-9 % et les enfants trouvés 1-2 % des naissances enregistrées dans la capitale. Dans les années de crise économique et de catastrophes naturelles, on observe un léger accroissement du nombre des enfants illégitimes et une forte augmentation du nombre des enfants abandonnés (de 1-2 % à 6-7 %). Il faut ajouter que parmi les enfants trouvés, les filles étaient les plus nombreuses (90 H/100 F).

Le problème de l'abandon des nourrissons dans la ville préindustrielle avait, à côté de l'aspect moral et juridique, un aspect strictement économique et démographique. D'un côté, la famille devait supporter les frais et les difficultés liés à l'éducation des enfants, d'un autre côté, les enfants constituaient une sorte d'aide et de main-d'œuvre et ils étaient une assurance pour la vieillesse des parents.

Dans les familles varsoviennes reconstituées, l'intervalle entre la date du mariage et la date de naissance du premier enfant (sans excepter les conceptions prénuptiales) était de 9-11 mois. Les enfants suivants venaient au monde tous les deux ans, mais l'intervalle entre les accouchements se réduisait à 20 mois si l'enfant précédent était mort avant d'avoir atteint l'âge d'un an. Les intervalles avant le dernier accouchement étaient plus longs – plus de 3 ans. Pendant les 12 premiers mois de la vie, la mort éliminait plus de 30 % des enfants et seulement 40-45 % d'entre eux atteignaient l'âge de 20 ans.

L'étude détaillée des facteurs biologiques qui influencent le nombre d'enfants au sein des familles varsoviennes démontre une diminution du nombre d'enfants au cours du XVIIIe siècle selon l'âge de la femme au moment du mariage et plus particulièrement une diminution de la fécondité légitime des mères de tous les groupes d'âge au sein des familles fondées dans les dernières années du XVIIIe siècle. Naturellement le nombre d'enfants était plus grand dans les familles dont la vie commune était plus longue et qui pouvaient donc mettre mieux à profit les possibilités de procréation de la femme. La fécondité diminuait progressivement avec la durée de l'union, en raison de l'épuisement de la femme causé par des maternités répétées. En même temps, la diminution de la fécondité dans les familles fondées à l'époque des Lumières (1770-1799) est nettement visible. On remarque déjà ce trait caractéristique au cours des cinq premières années du mariage, sans tenir compte de l'âge de la mère au moment du mariage. Dans les familles reconstituées fermées complètes, on ne note pas de tendance à l'exploitation maximale des possibilités de procréation. Les Varsoviennes mariées avant l'âge de 20 ans avaient en moyenne 33-34 ans lors de leur dernière maternité et celles mariées à l'âge de 20-24 ans avaient leur dernier accouchement 4 ans plus tard, donc longtemps avant le début de l'infécondité biologique.

Les résultats des recherches permettent de contester la thèse assez répandue d'une fécondité illimitée à l'époque préindustrielle à l'est de l'Elbe. Il semble donc que certaines familles varsoviennes pratiquaient le contrôle des naissances déjà à la fin du XVIIIe siècle. Il est utile de faire remarquer que la paroisse étudiée était habitée par beaucoup de familles de marchands, de fonctionnaires et de la noblesse. En effet, d'après des études solidement documentées effectuées en Europe occidentale, on peut affirmer que les processus de maternité voulue se sont présentés plus tôt dans les couches sociales les plus riches, et surtout dans les groupes de la bourgeoisie qui était en train de se former. Les présentes conclusions exigent évidemment d'autres études qui viendraient les confirmer. Nous avons l'intention de poursuivre les recherches sur la société de la Varsovie préindustrielle et sur la vie économique, en passant de l'étude verticale – évolutionnaire – à l'étude horizontale – structurale – qui permettra peut-être à l'avenir de présenter la fécondité des mariages et la mortalité à un degré supérieur dans la stratification sociale et professionnelle.

LE COMMERCE ET LE CAPITAL MERCANTILES A MAJORQUE, 1720-1800

CARLES MANERA

L'objet de cette étude est d'établir les données de base des échanges commerciaux pratiqués par les Majorquins au cours du XVIIIe siècle.

L'analyse des sources consultées permet de restituer quelques balances commerciales dans leur contexte. Elle démontre que d'une part, les denrées comestibles (l'huile en premier lieu) et les matières textiles constituent les principales ressources de l'île et que, d'autre part, les céréales, les produits manufacturés, les matières premières et les produits coloniaux représentent l'essentiel des cargaisons importées à Majorque.

L'évolution du trafic commercial se résume en trois phases.

1. Entre 1704 et 1750, c'est l'espace méditerranéen qui prédomine et essentiellement Gênes et Marseille. La relation avec ces ports se fait plus étroite à partir de 1730, ainsi qu'en témoignent les prix peu élevés de l'huile insulaire sur les marchés de ces deux villes. Ce sont les marins majorquins, il faut le souligner, qui contrôlent la navigation le long de ces routes commerciales traditionnelles et qui en retirent donc le bénéfice du fret.

2. Au cours de la période comprise entre 1750 et 1780, les échanges s'orientent vers les villes nord-atlantiques : Amsterdam et Londres absorbent le quart des exportations de l'île. Ces relations s'effectuent sous pavillons anglais, danois et hollandais. Elles se caractérisent très souvent par des expéditions peu nombreuses mais de grande capacité.

3. Finalement, de 1780 à 1800, on assiste à un recul du marché 'étranger' – dont la chute est progressive à partir de 1790 – en faveur des marchés péninsulaires et régionaux. C'est à cette époque que se situe l'ouverture légale du port de Palma aux colonies américaines, en même temps que se consolident les contacts établis antérieurement par les négociants majorquins.

L'évolution du commerce montre combien l'établissement d'infrastructures commerciales en Méditerranée et dans l'Atlantique influence de manière décisive l'écoulement des produits majorquins sur ces marchés. On constate ainsi l'adoption par les commerçants d'une stratégie rationnelle en politique économique : information soignée, rapidité des transactions, réduction des coûts et flexibilité dans l'investissement. L'application de tels principes suppose l'obtention de bénéfices accumulés au cours de diverses opérations à petite échelle plutôt qu'au cours de grandes affaires réalisées à court terme; en définitive, il s'agit d'une ascension sociale consécutive à une longue trajectoire économique.

Le déroulement de cette stratégie s'observe dans trois familles de grands commerçants : les Billon, les Marcel et les Capo. Les deux premières se rencontrent en une *première génération* qui, aux alentours des années 1750-1760, commerce en Méditerranée et dans l'Atlantique Nord, sans refuser l'éventualité d'aller jusqu'en Amérique par l'intermédiaire de Cadix ou des Canaries. Les Capo forment une *seconde génération* qui s'enrichit à la fin du XVIIIe siècle grâce à son intense activité commerciale sur les marchés traditionnels de l'île et à ses expéditions directes vers les colonies américaines. Ces deux générations présentent des traits communs : diversification des investissements dans des affaires très variées et intérêt porté à l'achat de terres en vue d'en retirer le fermage. La démarche économique de ces nouveaux riches est assez semblable à celle de l'aristocratie : ils recherchent des rentes sûres, afin de bénéficier de revenus fixes que les transactions mercantiles n'assurent pas toujours.

Il apparaît donc urgent de rejeter l'image d'une Majorque isolée, peu préparée aux activités commerciales, cliché qui a contribué à la vision d'un niveau mercantile critique au XVIIIe siècle. Au contraire, on peut parler d'un commerce décentralisé dépendant de l'activité du port de Palma et de ses relations avec les autres ports. L'impulsion donnée par le capital flottant favorise un grand éventail de transactions.

Je crois que l'on peut donc nuancer l'idée d'une économie majorquine déficitaire de façon permanente en raison d'un déséquilibre de la balance commerciale. Cette conception était propagée de propos délibéré par la classe intellectuelle et par la noblesse afin de présenter les marchands comme responsables de cette situation déplorable. Cet argument a servi aux aristocrates pour se présenter, à partir de 1780, comme l'unique secteur social réellement capable de stimuler des échanges et de débloquer le retard agricole, industriel et commercial, conséquence, selon eux, d'une gestion peu heureuse de la part des négociants.

Cependant les déficits ne sont pas éternels, surtout quand certains indices – comme la démographie – montrent de légères récupérations, et ils finissent par se résoudre. Ce schéma immobiliste présente le XVIIIe siècle comme une époque de faible activité économique : inconsistance des manufactures, inactivité portuaire, inexpérience des commerçants à établir des contacts à l'intérieur comme à l'extérieur, la réelle croissance de la population majorquine, plus importante d'ailleurs à la campagne que dans la capitale. Deux voies de recherche, encore à approfondir, peuvent contribuer à une interprétation différente de l'activité économique insulaire, tant externe qu'interne.

1. *Il faut étudier les variables de la balance commerciale sans perdre de vue celle des paiements, bien qu'il soit malaisé d'estimer l'état de celle-ci par manque de données.* Il est particulièrement difficile de déterminer les transferts invisibles de capitaux. Si l'on suppose un déséquilibre chronique de la balance commerciale, il faut le compenser par un autre type d'opérations économiques qui, par exemple, permettent d'expliquer rationnellement les achats, à l'extérieur, de quantités massives de céréales et de denrées comestibles (marchandises prioritaires pour la subsistance de l'île, bien que l'augmentation de la production de légumes pallie le manque de blé) ou les *inputs* de matières industrielles et textiles nécessaires au fonctionnement de l'infrastructure manufacturière. Il y a deux possibilités :

a) les gains sur les frets et sur les activités liées au crédit (assurances, transactions de lettres de change) réduisent les marges déficitaires. Le commerce en Méditerranée est contrôlé par les navigants locaux qui disposent d'une flotte de navires légers, de 20 à 50 tonneaux (quelquefois jusqu'à 100 tonneaux pour les voyages aux colonies) qui permettent le cabotage, des traversées rapides et de multiples contacts d'une côte à l'autre. Un trafic fluide garantit la rapidité du transport des marchandises et la certitude de s'octroyer une quantité plus importante de frets. On trouve l'inverse pour l'Atlantique Nord, là où les frets ne sont pas au chapitre 'recettes', le transport étant effectué par des bateaux étrangers qui chargent les marchandises à Palma. D'un autre côté, les assurances et les échanges maritimes représentent des formes de crédit qui, utilisées par les marchands et par d'autres groupes sociaux, apportent de l'argent liquide. Les bénéfices varient, selon les ports et les conjonctures politiques, entre 2 et 75 % du capital investi.

b) Les transferts de capitaux sont aussi compensatoires. L'exemple du trafic avec l'Amérique est éloquent et représentatif d'opérations similaires en différents endroits. Il est possible d'en mesurer la valeur : les navires avec participation majorquine en provenance des 'Indes' versaient aux douanes de Cadix et de Santa Cruz de Ténérife des sommes considérables en comparaison de celles payées au port de Palma. Entre 1787 et 1813 on compte près de 8 millions de réaux (*reales*) sur la place andalouse et plus d'un million sur celle de Santa Cruz, tandis qu'à Palma on n'enregistre que 344.896 réaux. Ceci ne veut pas dire que les deux premiers montants correspondent au gain de commerçants majorquins – l'absence de noms ne permet pas de s'en assurer – mais il n'est pas aventureux de supposer qu'il leur en revient une partie, en tant que résultat de négoces aux colonies. Les possibilités d'investissement de ces capitaux sont diverses : achat de marchandises pour l'Amérique ou pour la péninsule ibérique, acquisition de céréales et de produits manufacturés sur le littoral méditerranéen pour Majorque, endossement de lettres de change sur d'autres centres commerciaux très significatifs : Barcelone, Madrid, Marseille. De plus, une partie de leurs montant est 'rapatriée' sous forme d'effets commerciaux ou de numéraire. En tout cas, les opérations décrites génèrent des transactions internationales signifiant de nouveaux gains, qui, une fois ramenés à Majorque, deviennent un facteur d'équilibre de l'économie.

2. *Les données relatives à l'exportation ont confirmé un point qui n'est pas nouveau – la prédominance de l'huile – mais elles soulignent en même temps la présence notoire et d'une valeur non négligeable des matières textiles de production locale, à base de laine, de lin et d'un mélange de coton.* Certaines activités non agricoles, telles que la confection de chapeaux et de bérets de laine, de toile de lin ou de produits de filatures, sont donc significatives. Elles doivent être examinées d'un point de vue plus qualitatif que quantitatif, car elles permettent aux secteurs sociaux les plus défavorisés de disposer d'un revenu additionnel. Ces travaux sont effectués par des femmes et des journaliers, pendant leur temps libre. Les artisans les plus pauvres y participent également, en se soustrayant au contrôle rigoureux des corporations. On peut estimer que 14 à 15 %

de l'ensemble de la population majorquine appartient à cette catégorie de travailleurs non agricoles à temps partiel.

Les petits commerçants, stimulés par le faible coût d'opportunité, organisent ce type d'industrie domestique en deux phases. D'une part ils chargent un grand commerçant d'acheter les matières premières nécessaires (ou ils les acquièrent sur le marché local), matières qu'ils paient à crédit; d'autre part, ils livrent la matière première aux artisans, collectent les produits manufacturés à partir de celle-ci et les placent sur le marché intérieur et/ou chargent un négociant de les commercialiser à l'extérieur de l'île. C'est donc l'application du système du *putting out* (*Verlagsystem*). Cependant, il est également possible que les artisans contrôlent les *inputs* textiles et vendent leurs produits manufacturés aux commerçants, si bien que l'on se trouve alors devant les mécanismes du *Kaufsystem.*

Il reste encore deux questions qui serviront de conclusions générales.

1. *La théorie de croissance économique défendue par les intellectuels locaux, sous l'influence des ministres réformistes de l'époque bourbonnienne, ne se concrétise pas à Majorque.* Cependant, ce que nous savons de l'évolution économique de l'île au XVIIIe siècle, d'après l'analyse des indicateurs démographiques, de la production de céréales, d'huile, de légumes et du volume du commerce, nous permet d'affirmer l'existence de transformations internes. Il convient cependant de ne pas les associer à la prétendue volonté de changement des intellectuels aristocrates de la seconde moité du siècle. Il est bien évident, par exemple, qu'un des instruments fondamentaux de la consolidation de la puissance économique réside dans la capacité de placer les productions locales sur les marchés extérieurs et surtout dans la dynamisation du commerce direct avec l'Amérique. Les aristocrates qui, à la fin du siècle, forment à cet effet une compagnie commerciale, avec un capital initial de plus de 100.000 livres, non seulement ne participent pas à la nouvelle entreprise dans les circuits mercantiles, mais encore n'apparaissent que rarement sur la liste des négociants intéressés par la route des 'Indes'. En même temps, leur récession commerciale se vérifie dans l'ensemble des échanges du port de Palma. Le trafic colonial direct n'est cependant pas significatif dans le cas de Majorque car il ne concerne qu'un groupe bien particulier de négociants.

Le commerce des Majorquins avec les pays d'outre-mer, il ne faut pas l'oublier, se fait indirectement, au départ d'autres places portuaires.

2. *Ce ne sont pas les milieux aristocratiques et réformistes qui créent des fissures dans la structure socio-économique pour provoquer de grandes altérations.* En général, leurs théories sont prétentieuses mais leurs réalisations ne sont pas très effectives et se réduisent à de petites améliorations qui ne font absolument pas trembler les piliers de l'économie majorquine. De plus, l'oligarchie voit avec appréhension l'ascension progressive de groupes mercantiles qui peu à peu contrôlent les finances, les revenus fiscaux, les échanges, les mécanismes de crédit, en un mot le fonctionnement du marché. Cependant les grands commerçants, une fois propriétaires de la terre, adopteront une attitude socio-économique semblable à celle des nobles, de façon à réaliser leur objectif primordial : s'intégrer en tant que classe dominante au système de l'ancien régime. Les changements dans l'économie majorquine au XVIIIe siècle sont attribuables aux paysans, aux artisans, aux petits commerçants; elles sont dues également aux premières phases d'accumulation de richesse de ceux qui deviendront par la suite les plus grands marchands. Le comportement économique de ces groupes se caractérise par un dynamisme et une mobilité qui facilitent les relations entre les aires géographiques intérieures, les spécialisations industrielles et agricoles, la naissance d'infrastructures manufacturières et les rapports constants avec le monde extérieur.

La conjonction de facteurs internes (en relation avec la production et son organisation) et externes (les échanges, qui impliquent une solide connaissance des oscillations des marchés) et d'autres forces sociales comme moteurs déterminants, expliquent en définitive l'insertion de l'île dans les principaux circuits mercantiles.

STUDIES IN THE HISTORY OF SWEDISH FOOD CONSUMPTION: FOOD CONSUMPTION AMONG INSTITUTIONALLY SUPPORTED PAUPERS, 1621-1872

MATS MORELL

INTRODUCTION

In international research on food consumption and living standard in Western Europe since the Middle Ages, a 'Malthusian' view has been predominant. It has been claimed that meat consumption and food standards rose following the decrease of population after the Black Death. From around 1450, when population pressure set in again, diets got more and more dominated by cereals and coarser food stuffs, and the standard of nutrition deteriorated. This process continued well into the 18th century (Braudel, 1979, pp. 66-67, 127-134; Abel, 1980; Le Roy Ladurie, 1980).

Heckscher pointed at an increased prevalence of vegetable foods in Sweden as well from the 16th to the early 19th century (Heckscher, 1935-1949). The critique of Heckscher (cf. Morell, 1987) only slightly modified his conclusions. The same goes for most of the other contributions (e.g. Utterström, 1978).

Embarking from the state of research, the hypothesis of this investigation, aiming at an analysis of food consumption in Sweden in the early modern era, are the following.

1. The diet was characterized by *storage economy.* Little fresh food was served. Food was mainly dried or salted. The diet was one-sided and dominated by grain products.
2. The *level of consumption* and the *diet standard* deteriorated in the long run, at least up to the early 19th century.
3. The proportion of *vegetable foods* (*especially cereals*) *in the diet* increased up to the early 19th century.

THE INVESTIGATED POPULATIONS

Most specifically I have studied institutionally supported paupers, dwelling in Swedish 'hospitals' in 1621-1872. These institutions traced their origins back to the leprosy asylums and the Houses of the Holy Spirit of the Middle Ages, but in the 16th century they were transformed into asylums for paupers, invalids, the mentally ill and elderly people. The hospitals soon became centrally governed, integrated parts of the general policy towards paupers. From the mid 18th century onwards they slowly turned into asylums purely for the mentally ill. This is the connotation of the word 'hospital' today in the Swedish language.

I have chosen three hospitals on the northern shore of lake Mälaren – Västerås (1621-1823), Enköping (1759-1781), Weckholm (1696-1872) – and Falu hospital (1659-1837) in the copper mine town of Falun in Dalarna county. Crown tithes in grain formed the bulk of these hospitals' incomes. Detailed accounts of weekly or monthly provisions allow us to create long and continuous time series concerning per capita food consumption among the inmates.

Weckholm's hospital held only 12 inmates, the three others 25-50. Females outnumbered males and most inmates were described as elderly, weak, invalids, mentally deranged or poor. Commonly they originated from lower class rural backgrounds, but there were always some people from higher classes in the hospitals: old priests, burghers, craftsmen and farmers. The inmates (or their home parishes) had to pay considerable fees to be let in. Clearly hospital inmates were privileged compared to other paupers.

THE INMATES' DIET

80-95 % of the energy in the inmates' diet was derived from vegetable sources; 60-70 % of the energy, in Enköping even 80 %, originated from cereals. The food was very low in fat (6-10 % of the energy) and rich in carbohydrates (70-80 %).

The diet was based upon rye bread, gruels, porridges and beer. The menus were enrichened with vegetables, fish, meat and small amounts of milk and butter. The beef being served three or four times a week, was usually soaked in a salty brine or dried and mixed in a soup with cabbage, turnips, peas or cereals. Not much pork or mutton was eaten. Salted (mainly Baltic) herring and dried cod were staple foods in the hospitals. Salted fish was usually eaten uncooked, dried fish was soaked before cooking. Almost all the food eaten had been preserved for a long time.

The diet was slightly altered according to season. In summer more butter and milk was served, instead of dried fish. Turnips and cabbage replaced some of the peas in autumn and early winter. Fresh vegetables and fruits may have reached the inmates' tables in late summer.

The range of different food elements dwindled over the centuries. The assortment of fish in Västerås and Falun diminished during the 17th century. Dried fish disappeared from the Falun menu in 1813. The little fresh meat and entrail foods (sausages, blood, liver) previously provided during autumn disappeared as the hospitals ceased buying oxen for slaughter and instead bought prepared meat. In Västerås fruit, carrots and green vegetables were spoken of only in the 1620's, and wheat bread appears in no menu after 1735. Among new features potatoes were served regularly in Falun from 1813 onwards, and from 1826 in Västerås. Turnips, became a regular item in Falun by 1813. Onions and oatmeal were served in Falun from 1826. Generally speaking, the diet turned less and less diversified during the studied centuries. Predominantly animal food elements disappeared.

LONG TERM QUANTITATIVE CHANGES IN THE INMATES' FOOD CONSUMPTION

Data from all four institutions exists only for 1759-1781. Table 1 shows per capita consumption of different foods in this period.

Table 1 : *Annual per capita provisioning of different foods in the four hospitals. Averages for 1759-1781*

Food group	Enköping	Falun	Weckholm	Västerås	4 hospitals
Grain	330	292	283	365	318
Vegetables	56	32	40	44	43
Meat incl. entrails	19	34	16	40	27
Fish	14	83	43	46	46
Butter	0	5	1	6	3
Milk	0	10	8	8	6

Sources: Accounts from the hospitals of Enköping, Falun, Weckholm and Västerås (Districal archive of Uppsala, County museum of Västmanland, archive of the cathedral chapter in Västerås, National archive, Stockholm).

For Weckholm few long term changes can be discerned, but consumed quantities stabilized on earlier peak levels from the mid 18th century. Enköping we can disregard in the following. Otherwise a long term growth in the consumption of vegetable foodstuffs is evident. Consumption of vegetables and root crops grew in Västerås from the 1630's onwards, in Falun up to 1700 and from the 1810's onwards and in Weckholm during the 1730's. Total grain consumption tended to rise from the 1630's to 1810 in Västerås and from 1659 to the 1780's in Falun. Among cereals rye gained relative importance in Västerås in the 1620's and in the latter part of the 17th and early part of the 18th century. The same was true for Falun, but only by the end of the 18th century. Consumption of barley, mainly used for brewing, diminished in Västerås during the 17th century. In Falun consumption rose 1750-1786, but dwindled from 1804 onwards.

The consumption of animal food stuffs tended to decrease, even though the picture is not very clear. With a few exceptions (Västerås in 1722-1736 and Falun in 1826-1837) consumption of milk and butter, was insignificant, although it tended to increase on long term. In Västerås meat consumption fell in 1621-1645, rose in the 1650's and fell again in the 1690's. It started to rise by 1720, but fell permanently in the 1770's. In Falun meat consumption fell abruptly in 1700-1730, during the 1750's and in the 1810's. The consumption of fish grew in Västerås up to the 1650's, but diminished sharply during the later half of the 17th century. Consumption rose later but never to reach again the 17th century levels. In Falun fish-consumption diminished from 1674 to 1720, but thereafter it increased until 1760. Finally it fell stepwise; by 1826 it was insignificant. In Weckholm fish tended to replace meat from the 1740's onwards. Meat rations decreased around 1810.

The decades around the year 1700 appear as a period of food crisis in the hospitals of Falun, Weckholm and Västerås. Per capita consumption of practically all food items decreased.

In the long run the proportion of the inmates' total energy intake derived from vegetable foods stuffs rose. This process appeared earlier in Västerås than in Falun and it was less evident in Weckholm. Similarly the share of animal protein out of all protein consumed diminished in Weckholm during the 1720's and 1740's. It rose in the 1750's but fell permanently around 1810. In Enköping this proportion fell in the 1770's. In Västerås it decreased from c. 50 % in the 1630's to roughly 30 % from the 1770's onwards. In Falun it fell by more than a third from 1756 to 1837.

THE INMATES' INTAKE OF ENERGY AND THEIR STANDARD OF NUTRITION

Conclusions concerning the adequacy of the per capita intake of energy and protein are summed up in tables 2 and 3.

Table 2: *The inmates' daily per capita energy intake compared to the requirements of a modern female reference person*

Hospital	Probably satisfactory	Probably not satisfactory	No safe conclusion possible
Enköping	1775-81	–	1759-74
Falun	1740,1746,1772, 1786-1814,1822	(1663), 1720	all other years
Weckholm	–	1710, (1719), 1724,1727	all other years
Västerås	1627,1730, 1736-1823	–	all other years

Sources: See table 1.

Table 3: The inmates daily per capita protein intake compared to the requirements of a modern female reference person

Hospital	Probably satisfactory	Probably not satisfactory	No safe conclusion possible
Enköping	1759-81	–	–
Falun	all years except 1720	(1720)	(1720)
Weckholm	1701-09, 1712, 1714 1716-18, 1720-22, 1731, 1737-42, 1744, 1749, 1754-1872	1710, (1719), (1724), (1727)	all other years
Västerås	1621-36, 1639-54, 1657-59, 1663, 1665-66, 1670-74, 1678-89, 1693-96, 1700-02, 1723-1823	–	all other years

Sources: See table 1.

The impression of a food crisis in the decades around the year 1700, i.e. during the Great Nordic War, is reinforced by the analysis of the energy and protein intake. It shall be noted that intake of energy was also low in Västerås in 1675-76 and in many years between 1688 and 1720. From c. 1730 the levels of energy and protein consumed stabilized. It is not likely that per capita intake of energy was too low in any of these institutions after 1730. Similarly, from 1753 onwards the proetin intake was on acceptable levels in all the institutions investigated. The individual intake of energy was always comparatively high in Västerås (c. 2600 kcal a day in the period 1759-81) and comparatively low in Weckholm (around 2000 kcal in 1759-81). In Enköping it rose from 2300 kcal to 2500 kcal, and in Falun it fluctuated between 2100 and 2500 kcal a day per capita during the same years.

The intake of vitamins of the B-complex seems to have been sufficient and the same may with some reservation be true for iron. The intake of vitamins A and D as well as of calcium appears to have been far too low. The same is true for the intake of ascorbic acid (vitamin C). The situation improved when potatoes started to be served regularly from 1812 in Falun and from 1826 in Västerås.

Apart from the diet being unsatisfactory with respect to certain nutrients, the low fat content may have led to a 'bulk problem' : to satisfy energy needs, food had to be served in very large portions, and it is questionable whether the inmates managed to eat it all. Thus, in practice energy requirements may not have been fulfilled, although rations seemed to be adequate.

EXPLANATORY DISCUSSION

My results concerning hospital diets support to some degree the 'vegetabilization' hypothesis (≠ 3 above), but although the animal content in diets and their variation decreased, the view that dietary standards in general deteriorated (≠ 2) is not fully confirmed. Hypothesis ≠ 1 fully fits with my results; hospital diets differed from diets of other large households only by depending more on cereals, namely rye.

The fact that the hospitals were supported by generous amounts of grain from tithes may have led the authorities which were responsible for the composition of the diets to make more use of cereals than was otherwise common. In normal years grain allowances to the hospitals were large enough to render storage and even speculation in grain prices possible. Together with the rarely altered food budgets this accounts for an overall stability of the alimentation in the hospitals. The crisis of the early 18th century may be explained by successive years of disastrous harvests that affected the volume of tithe grain delivered, and by difficulties – due to the war – to procure other food items.

It is known that rye production rose at the expense of barley production from the 16th century onwards, and it is likely that, by the period covered in this investigation, this process had developed further in the region of lake Mälaren, from which Västerås hospital was provided with grain, than it had in the area further to the northwest which supplied Falu hospital. Through the tithes, changes in the proportions of the different grains cultivated were reflected in the diets of the hospitals.

Prices of vegetable foodstuffs rose in comparison to those for animal foodstuffs during the 18th century. This seems to speak for the Malthusian case with regard to Sweden as well. It is difficult however, to see why these relative price changes should have prompted the authorities responsible for composing the hospital diets to a relative increase in the consumption of cereals. Thanks to the price changes, the hospitals could earn more from selling parts of their stable and large incomes in grains and procure more meat etc. It thus seems that in an indirect way, the hospital diets were influenced by the popular diet in general; if the cereal proportion of the latter increased, those authorities composing the inmates' menus changed the hospital diets in the same manner, albeit with some delay.

Cultural influences from the Catholic church which was estabished in Sweden during the Middle Ages should not be ruled out. If monasteries were strongholds of a specially designed ritual diet (bread, cheese and wine), the early hospitals, with their monastery-like rules, could have been so too. Medieval hospital menus confirm this, and reminiscences of the fasting days are found in the menus well into the 17th century. Perhaps this tradition, together with the hospitals' specific types of income, explain why hospital diets were heavily dominated by grain products, before popular diets in general became so. All in all hospital diets were somewhat peculiar and there are, as we have seen, many reasons why our knowledge about them cannot be generalized without considerable care.

Certain ethnologists (notably Campbell, 1950; Olsson, 1958 and Ränk, 1966) emphasize the importance of the slow, steady work of cultural diffusion (see for the impact of ritually sanctioned food habits upon agriculture in Western Europe, Duby, 1976A, pp. 191-195; Duby, 1976B, pp. 23-27, 31-32 and Teuteberg, 1986). Open field agriculture and bread culture spread from the high Middle Ages onwards and following land reclamation, an older lacto-animalic diet was suppressed northwards. Maybe we must acknowledge that the long term development of diet in Sweden was part of a process by which the country was drawn into a new culture, which was defined by a certain pattern of production, certain methods of cultivating the fields and corresponding diary habits. This cultural pattern may have spread due to the working of a complicated set of economic and ideologic factors, which cannot be reduced to a few economic-theoretical statements. We can see that its penetration of Scandinavia took long time and that the bread culture achieved regional peculiarities. Bread culture and village agriculture reached its peak in Sweden in the 18th century.

By then it was close to its limits of expansion. Later on, enclosure movements, the agrarian revolution, potatoes and industrialization changed consumption patterns profoundly.

REFERENCES

W. Abel, *Agricultural Fluctuations in Europe. From the Thirteenth to the Twentieth Century* (London, 1980).

F. Braudel, *Civilization and Material life 1400-1800* (Bungay, 1979).

Å. Campbell, *Det svenska brödet. En jämförande etnologisk-historisk undersökning* (Stockholm, 1950).

G. Duby, 'Medieval Agriculture 900-1500', C.M. Cipolla, ed., *The Fontana Economic History of Europe. 1. The Middle Ages* (London, 1976). Cit. 1976 A.

G. Duby, *Krigare och Bönder. Den europeiska ekonomins första uppsving 600-1200* (Stockholm, 1976). Cit. 1976 B.

E.F. Heckscher, *Sveriges ekonomiska Historia från Gustav Vasa* (Stockholm, 1935-1949).

E. Le Roy Ladurie, *The Peasants of Languedoc* (Urbana, 1980).

M. Morell, 'Eli F. Heckscher, the "Food Budgets" and Swedish Food Consumption from the 16th to the 19th Century. The Summing up and Conclusions of a Long Debate', *The Scandinavian Economic History Review,* 35, 1 (1987).

A. Olsson, *Om allmogens kosthåll. Studier med utgångspunkt från västnordiska kostvanor* (Göteborg, 1958).

G. Ränk, *Från mjölk till ost. Drag ur den äldre mjölkhushållningen i Sverige* (Lund, 1966).

H.J. Teuteberg, 'Periods and Turning-Points in the History of European Diet: A Preliminary Outline of Problems and Methods', A. Fenton and E. Kisbàn, eds., *Food in Change. Eating Habits from the Middle Ages to the Present Day* (Edinburgh, 1986).

G. Utterström, *Fattig och föräldralös i Stockholm under 1600-och 1700-talen* (Umeå, 1978).

LA COURSE MAJORQUINE DANS LA MEDITERRANEE OCCIDENTALE, 1652-1698 UN COMMERCE FORCE

GONÇAL LÓPEZ NADAL

Ce travail fait partie d'un ample projet d'investigation sur les corsaires majorquins aux Temps Modernes. A ce premier stade, l'attention se concentre sur l'une des trois perspectives dans lesquelles doit se traiter l'étude globale du projet, à savoir les relations de la course insulaire avec les sociétés côtières de la Méditerranée occidentale. Les deux autres aspects décrits en détail dans le chapitre d'introduction, envisagent : a) la structure de la course et son explication comme véhicule commercial de la société dont elle est issue (Majorque) et b) les relations avec l'Etat qui la protège ainsi que la contribution de cette marine comme flotte auxiliaire de la Monarchie Catholique. Il s'agit donc ici d'étudier la course majorquine, en examinant son développement par rapport aux répercussions produites dans les sociétés qui, d'une manière ou d'une autre, ont été inévitablement obligées de supporter les déprédations des corsaires insulaires.

Le travail utilise une documentation étendue et dispersée qui m'a obligé à me déplacer pour consulter différentes archives espagnoles, italiennes et françaises dont quelques unes sont conservées dans les ports qui ont connu directement les effets de la course. Cette documentation se complète d'une ample bibliographie spécialisée en histoire économique maritime.

La thèse se divise en trois parties qui envisagent respectivement les relations avec la France, avec les états italiens et avec les pays barbaresques. Les deux premières parties sont divisées en chapitres. Pour les relations avec la France, ces chapitres correspondent aux différentes routes commerciales touchées; pour l'Italie, ils sont consacrés aux rapports avec un état ou un port déterminé. En ce qui concerne l'Afrique du Nord, au contraire, il s'agit d'un tout, avec comme seules divisions celles qui impliquent un changement thématique important. Un point sur lequel j'insiste énormément est celui de l'interrelation entre les sociétés envisagées. C'est une chose dont il faut spécialement tenir compte pour saisir les mouvements complexes qui se produisent dans le même environnement, à savoir la zone occidentale de la Méditerranée.

Les caractéristiques principales peuvent se synthétiser en différents points de la maniére suivante :

1. Dans la première partie, j'examine l'effet de la course majorquine sur le trafic commercial français. A cet égard, il faut considérer les deux circonstances qui facilitent et qui déterminent cet impact : d'une part, la situation de conflit quasi ininterrompue entre la France et l'Espagne pendant la période étudiée; d'autre part l'importance du réseau commercial existant entre les ports français, spécialement celui de Marseille, et les centres névralgiques de l'économie méditerranéenne. La convergence de ces deux facteurs explique le rapide processus de développement de la course majorquine, l'extraordinaire transformation qui la fait passer d'un niveau 'artisanal' à celui d'une authentique entreprise. Les navires marchands français sont sans nul doute la proie principale des corsaires insulaires. Leurs interceptions se succèdent sur toutes les routes commerciales françaises, tant celles de la 'mer intérieure' – c'est-à-dire le commerce de port à port et les lignes italienne, espagnole, barbaresque et levantine –, que celles de l'Atlantique – la 'façade ponentaise' selon Gaston Rambert – puisque l'on observe la prise de bateaux malouins chargés de morue, qui pénètrent en Méditerranée. En définitive, le commerce français était très notoirement affecté.

Dans cette partie, j'analyse les divers aspects de l'histoire de la course, depuis ce qui concerne la capture elle-même – combats, persécutions, intimidations ... – jusqu'aux réactions qui se produisent au sein de la Chambre de Commerce de Marseille qui était l'organisme responsable de la navigation commerciale française dans la Méditerranée. J'étudie les témoignages des consuls de Sa Majesté Très Chrétienne dans les principaux ports italiens et dans les échelles du Levant et leurs tentatives, peu couronnées de succès, d'éviter ces attaques.

D'une manière générale, il est intéressant d'analyser les pertes subies par le commerce marseillais pendant la Guerre de la Ligue d'Augsbourg; ces pertes sont dues à des 'accidents naturels' ('naufrages, incendies, échouements, saisies, pertes, sinistres, revoltes, fracassements, arrestements, coulebas, abandonnements, enlevements (et) enterrements'). Durant ce conflit, connu également comme la 'Guerre de Neuf Ans' (1689-1698), les corsaires majorquins s'emparèrent de 54 embarcations (48 françaises, 3 gênoises et 1 savoyarde). Ce chiffre n'est inférieur que de deux unités à celui des prises attribuées à la flotte de guerre anglaise, officiellement belligérante. Les corsaires majorquins, en Méditerranée, dépassent ceux des Provinces-Unies (Hollandais et Zélandais principalement) et même les redoutables corsaires barbaresques d'Alger, de Tunis ou de Tripoli.

Par conséquent, les dommages causés par les corsaires insulaires, qui ne sont surpassés en nombre de captures que par la toute puissante 'Royal Navy', montrent bien le rôle surprenant de ces équipages de particuliers et leur impact nuisible sur le commerce français dans la Méditerranée.

2. Dans la deuxième partie, j'étudie les contacts, tout différents, avec les états indépendants d'Italie. En prévision de prochains travaux, j'ai volontairement omis l'étude des relations avec la Sardaigne, avec Naples et avec la Sicile, royaumes intégrés dans l'appareil administratif de la Monarchie Catholique. Je consacre cependant quelques pages à l'analyse du rôle important du petit port de Finale, enclave sur la côte ligurienne, position stratégique pour les opérations de la course majorquine dans la région.

La plupart des pages de cette partie sont dédiées à l'étude de la répercussion de la course majorquine sur l'économie de deux ports neutres : Gênes et Livourne. Ces deux villes politiquement indépendantes s'efforcent de ne pas intervenir dans les guerres franco-espagnoles de la deuxième moitié du XVIIe siècle. Pourtant, les prétentions et les succès sont très différents dans l'un et l'autre cas. Cette situation se reflète dans les effets, nettement opposés, de la présence des corsaires majorquins dans les deux ports. Les Majorquins se réfugient dans les ports de la 'Signoria' face à la pression de la marine royale française. Les protestations des autorités gênoises n'amènent pas la diminution des opérations corsaires, stimulées par l'important trafic qui liait les foires de Beaucaire avec celles de Pise. La réplique française ne se fait pas attendre. La politique répressive de la république de Gênes entraîne des représailles envers ses sujets dans le port de Majorque. Une politique de neutralité si malhabilement menée ne produit que des résultats négatifs.

Pour Livourne les choses sont totalement différentes. L'utilisation efficace de la disposition qui transformait la ville portuaire toscane en port franc faisait que les Majorquins, comme les autres corsaires – des Napolitains aux Nordiques de Flessingue – s'y présentaient avec d'autres intentions. Ils y venaient soit pour vendre leurs prises, de manière à ne pas devoir les remorquer jusqu'à leur port d'origine, soit pour réparer les avaries produites par des attaques ou des tempêtes. Sous la protection de cette neutralité, bien mieux administrée que celle de Gênes, les corsaires avaient l'avantage de pouvoir compter sur un refuge où ils pouvaient préparer leurs plans de campagne. De leur côté, les négociants de Livourne savaient profiter de ces visites et tiraient de grands bénéfices de l'achat des captures réalisées par les corsaires. On peut parler d'une certaine relation de symbiose entre marchands et corsaires : ceux-ci amenant leurs prises dont les premiers se portent acquéreurs. En réalité, ils se favorisent réciproquement : les corsaires, notamment les Majorquins, profitent de la neutralité livournaise, tandis que les marchands du port toscan, ceux qui contrôlent la circulation commerciale, augmentent leurs recettes avec le bénéfice de la course.

D'autres ports, comme ceux du duché de Savoie (Nice et Villefranche) et ceux de la république de Saint-Marc, eurent affaire aux corsaires majorquins, bien que dans une moindre mesure. Les rapports avec les deux premiers sont fréquents en raison de leur situation géographique entre la France et Gênes. La capture de bateaux marchands vénitiens doit être considérée comme une saisie de bâtiments navigant sous pavillon neutre. Il ne faut pas oublier le rôle de transporteurs de marchandises de la Sublime-Porte rempli par les Vénitiens. L'action des corsaires entraîna de dures représailles de la part des autorités vénitiennes sur les rares navires majorquins, corsaires ou non, qui pénétraient dans l'Adriatique. Pour cette raison, les relations entre corsaires et Vénitiens étaient peu cordiales puisqu'il était pratiquement impossible de rendre compatibles deux formes de navigation totalement dissemblables.

3. Les relations avec les pays barbareques sont difficiles à discerner. Cette situation est due au fait que les Barbaresques sont considérés comme des 'ennemis de la Foi'. Ils se distinguent ainsi irrémédiablement des adversaires politiques ou 'ennemis de la Couronne'. En effet, les relations avec les pays européens supposent une procédure institutionnelle – protestations, jugements, réclamations ... – tandis que la capture d'une embarcation barbaresque ne pose aucun problème : la prise est bien faite, un point c'est tout!

Au point de vue méthodologique, la structure de cette partie de mon travail se base sur l'analyse de différents points de vue, plus ou moins autonomes, mais intimement liés au phénomène corsaire.

3. A) *La course majorquine sur les côtes de 'Barbarie'.* En étudiant les diverses raisons qui conduisent les corsaires insulaires sur les littoraux du Maghreb, on peut distinguer quatre éléments déterminants :

1. Ceux de tendance politico-militaire, qui se traduisent en opérations punitives contre les ports nord-africains (spécialement Alger).
2. Les institutionnels que nous pouvons observer dans les ordonnances en vigueur sur la guerre de course.
3. Les religieux qui présentent nettement un aspect de croisade.
4. Les économiques, et plus spécialement la nécessité de se rendre dans ces régions pour acquérir du blé.

3. B) *Les captures.* Il faut distinguer entre les prises effectuées à l'intérieur des terres – comme celles réalisées par les Barbaresques lors de leurs incursions sur les côtes de l'archipel des Baléares et du Levant ibérique – et les prises proprement maritimes, fruits d'une attaque ou d'un combat entre corsaires. Dans ce paragraphe, en même temps que les captures attribuées aux Majorquins, ressortent celles réalisées par d'autres corsaires insulaires, ceux d'Ibiza.

3. C) *Les prisonniers.* Bien que l'origine de leur servitude soit la même, à savoir la prise en course, la figure de l'esclave 'maure' se distingue nettement de celle du captif chrétien. Il faut noter les conséquences sociales et économiques de l'inclusion du facteur humain comme objet prioritaire parmi les marchandises capturées par les corsaires des deux camps.

3. D) *La course majorquine et la course barbaresque.* On analyse ici l'interconnexion entre les deux courses, en évaluant leur rôle réciproque dans leurs processus respectifs de développement. Les effets sont notoirement paradoxaux. La course majorquine s'alimente de la barbaresque; pour cette dernière, les Majorquins représentent une des raisons de leurs progressive perte de capacité opérative, tant sur le plan militaire que commercial, durant la période étudiée.

Le sous-titre de la thèse résume les conclusions du travail. La pratique de la guerre de course en Méditerranée a pour effet de faire éclore différents procédés destinés à garantir, avec plus ou moins de chance, le maintien des relations commerciales. Il s'agit, clairement, d'un commerce forcé. Celui-ci présente un double sens : il implique premièrement d'importantes altérations sur les lignes commerciales régulières; en second lieu, il entraîne le développement commercial des neutres.

Examinons le premier point de vue en partant des transformations du système organisateur du commerce auxquelles ont abouti, par exemple, les Français. Les Majorquins, tout comme les corsaires d'autres régions – Espagnols, Italiens, Zélandais et Barbaresques – représentent un facteur de poids dans les réformes des marines marchande et militaire promues par Colbert. L'action des corsaires provoque également un renforcement de la surveillance sur les côtes franco-italiennes pour éviter l'effondrement du trafic. Les dispositions successives prises pour contenir leurs attaques, tout comme les moyens de les combattre, entraînent de fortes dépenses; les escortes, les convois etc. se révèlent finalement des remèdes coûteux et fragiles. L'emploi de l'Armée Royale sera, tout au plus, un dispositif occasionnel, généralement insuffisant. Le recours aux alliés de l'Afrique du Nord – en fait les corsaires barbaresques – peut très bien avoir un effet absolument contraire. La solution de l'utilisation des neutres finira par être coûteuse, sans être le moins du monde sûre. Malgré tous les efforts, les interceptions se sucèdent et affectent la totalité des lignes commerciales de la Méditerranée. Les captures deviennent un risque de première importance que doivent assumer les responsables du commerce maritime. En certaines occasions, face à la présence menaçante de galères corsaires, on jugeait prudent de rester à l'ancre dans le port. Sûrement, dans son ensemble, cette situation devait se traduire en certains effets positifs. Malgré cela, le coût de la lutte anticorsaire était très supérieur aux résultats les plus favorables. En définitive, le commerce subissait une véritable distorsion.

L'alternative du recours aux neutres obéit à la nécessité d'entretenir des relations commerciales fermes et garanties dans une conjoncture politique difficile. Cependant cette solution montrera rapidement certains défauts internes, difficiles à corriger, et ne sera plus un moyen de transport sûr. La méfiance qu'inspire logiquement le pavillon du pays neutre lui fera perdre son immunité face aux forces navales environnantes qui agissent avec la certitude d'obtenir quelque profit. Le prix du fret augmentera en peu de temps. En conséquence, le commerce de ces nations, surgi de la guerre, en sera finalement la victime : les corsaires, force navale, le créent, et les corsaires, comme moyen de guerre en mer, simplement le détruisent.

Les effets sont alors très évidents : pendant que la plupart des ports voient disparaître de nombreuses embarcations, d'autres ports – en minorité – s'enrichissent grâce à l'arrivée des prises effectuées par les corsaires. Certains vaisseaux français, ceux qui, par exemple, avaient levé l'ancre en direction de Livourne, pouvaient parvenir à ce port; mais, ils étaient entretemps passés sous le contrôle de corsaires majorquins! Le commerce avait violemment changé de mains.

ESTATES FOR SALE. THE REAL-ESTATE MARKET AND CHANGES IN LAND PROPERTY STRUCTURE OF GENTRY IN KALISZ COUNTY, 1580-1655

ANDRZEJ POŚPIECH

In the period under study, the trade in estates was one of the most important spheres of the gentry's economic activity. Enormous fortunes were accumulated by some efficient operators. These, however, were usually only individual, very well-to-do noblemen. This study proposes a different approach : the functional study of the real-estate trade within a limited territory and concerning an entire gentry community.

The main feature of the Polish land market of XVIth-XVIIth century was its total dominance by the nobility. The legal monopoly of ownership eliminated competitors from all other social classes and permitted total economic freedom in land alienations. On the other hand the land remained the basis of the *more nobilium* existence, while the lack of other socially permissible sources of income caused a more intensive struggle for land. The competition became even more acute since Polish law prescribed equal partition of inherited land among the sons. Thus, we are faced with the free market economy within one social estate, where the demand continuously outstrips the supply.

Two research perspectives are to be considered : the economic relations are infused with the social context of market phenomena. There is no sense in separating these factors, nor is it practically possible to do so. Their analysis must be simultaneous. However, it seems reasonable to view their impact on the mechanisms of land market.

One question to be asked is to what degree this market tended to react to economic factors (agricultural booms, monetary perturbations, etc.) and how did it escape its direct pressures? What made the market economy run and decide the rate of land traffic? Was profit always a decisive motive? Were interfamily transactions, formally resembling the acts of sale, really the exchange contracts?

A partial answer is attempted in the study of local real-estate market in Kalisz County in the period of 1580-1655. This example, concerning a relatively small area, provides sufficient grounds for general considerations. The economic wealth, and social structure of the region is representative for a much wider area of Poland, particularly its western region (Wielkopolska).

As everywhere else, the majority of the land belonged to the gentry. The nobles held over 80 % of the villages (316) and over 70 % of the cultivated soil, much more than all other landowners : the king, the clergy, or municipal governments. The gentry's agrarian economy was oriented mainly to grain production and less to animal farming. Estate owners employed their own labourers, peasants obliged to perform serf labour for their feudal over-lords. At the same time the social structure of the gentry was socially and economically balanced. The land property structure of the region was dominated by the middle-class gentry and the most diffuse type of real-estate was owned by this social group, as in the rest of Poland.

The study was based on a group of 1736 perpetual land alienation deeds. They survive in 13 volumes of *Libri Resignationum* of Kalisz County (belonging to *Acta Castrensis Calisiensis)* for the period of 1580-1655. The source basis is not complete, but it comprises over 75 % of the land alienation transactions performed in this area. This amount proved sufficient for the needs of analysis.

Each deed of land alienation included three elements. It named the object of the transaction, both of the contractors and, in the majority of cases, the sum paid in purchase. These elements determined the structure of the study. In the first part, entitled 'Gentry Estates' I surveyed the object of the transactions. Beginning with the settlement pattern, I reconstructed the system of stable economic ties between different localities. I also analyzed the mechanisms of growth, expansion, and decay of individual estates.

In the second part, entitled 'Prices and Value of Real-Estates' I turned to land-price movements and shifts in real-estate value over the studied period. The most important factors of price changes were the impact of economic booms, monetary fluctuations, and alterations in the amount of grain production.

The last part of the study was devoted to the individual and group behaviour of the gentry on the local land market. In this section, I surveyed, among other things, the economic policy of gentry families, the participation and market activity of various groups of local *possessores,* the efficacy of estate building, and the thresholds and barriers of advancement in local community.

The conclusions result from the parallel application of two methods : first the quantitative analysis of the entire body of source material, and, second, the numerous microanalytic procedures performed for every village in the region. The main conclusions are the following :

In the period of 1580-1655, there were 316 villages owned by gentry in Kalisz County. In the late XVIth century, they were divided into 529 individual estate units. This number fell to 413 in the mid-XVIIth century. The land-ownership pattern was dominated by the small area estates no larger than one village. Precise results were difficult to establish as the transaction deeds did not mention land measurement units and spoke only in such terms as *tota villa*, *pars villae*, *tota bona* etc.

The decrease by 22 % of the estates did not bring any fundamental changes in the economic structure of the county. The expansion or breakup of real-estate followed the domino pattern. Autonomous economic units, well established and functioning for considerable periods of time, were either attached or disconnected. They could be formed by larger or smaller land parcels, whole estates units, or in the case of extensive holdings, their separate parts.

Two opposite trends shaped the ownership relations in the County. First, there was the legally safeguarded necessity to distribute the estates equally among heirs. Second, successive generations consistently consolidated the estate anew. Those who initiated this process were usually the older co-heirs, although at times individuals from outside the family performed the same action, systematically buying up real-estate parcels from heirs. At least 40 % of the Kalisz County transactions were interfamilial and corrected the principle of equal distribution by adapting it to economic reality.

The tendency to reconstruct an estate marked mainly the middle gentry who were the most numerous in the region. Petty gentry of poorer status reacted the opposite way. They consistently subdivided their ever-shrinking estates over successive generations in order to maintain at all costs at least a substitute of possession.

Estate activity of cottage and petty gentry was dominated by individual horizons, while the middle class nobility acted with a much greater degree of group interest and conscious family policy. Their primary aim was the defence of the substance of the family estate and the maintenance of its social status. Due to the numerical superiority of middle-class gentry, these types of estate procedures shaped the wealth and economic structure of Kalisz County.

The activity of the gentry on the local real-estate market was inversly proportional to its place in the socio-economic structure. Cottagers and petty landowners were more numerous and active, yet this had no impact on their market efficiency. On the contrary, a symptom of the permanent crisis affecting this group, was its growing estate dispersion. The scale of their ownership decreased from 81 owned villages in the late XVIth century to 35 in the mid-XVIIth century. This indicates that these groups lost nearly 56 % of initial amount of owned land.

The middle class gentry, holding the estates from a half to three villages, gradually increased its hold by 12 % (from 188 to 210 villages). Most spectacular was the 51 % increase of ownership of extensive land holders (47 to 71 villages). However, from the social point of view, much more important was the steady decrease especially in petty gentry holdings and also in cottager holdings. This concerned a much larger group of land owners. This example shows the rapid impoverishment of the entire social classes which, in the later XVIIth century, were to disappear nearly entirely in Wielkopolska.

It is significant that the losses suffered by poorer gentry did not affect, as could be expected, the richest land holders. The middle-class gentry grew richer at the cost of their poorer neighbours while itself was the prey of the richest local landowners. The balance of mutual gains and losses of real-estate traffic for different strata of local gentry indicates that the flow of landed wealth was limited. Among 308 villages named in transaction deeds, only 68 (= 22 %) became the property of either rich or poor gentry.

The majority of trade contracts concerned members of each particular group. The partners belonged to the same social class and had a similar level of wealth. Hence, the local land market was highly diversified both socially and economically. We may even speak of several, socially isolated, land markets functioning at the same time, separated by the contractors' wealth level, the size of the real-estate, etc. Thus, the picture of the gentry's land market displays a similarity to the gentry marriage market.

The real-estate was worth as much as it brought in cash. Fixed and certain profit was guaranteed only in the case of a good harvest. The changes of land prices correlated with the price movements of crops indicate that the periods of fertility increased the value of land despite lower prices of grain. The years of dearth caused the opposite : land was cheap even if grain was expensive.

The level of prices and value of land, just like the gentry profits, depended mainly on the amount of crops gathered and on the increase or decrease of marketed grain production volume. The comparison of the real value of land and grain computed in silver indicates that the movement of land prices was connected to a much smaller degree with the fluctuations in grain price and the demand for agricultural products. The obtained results show an almost inversly proportional relation. On the other hand, the monetary perturbations very important for this period obviously affected the level of nominal land prices, but their impact on the real value changes of land was also only marginal.

The same mechanism regulated the rate of land transactions, the number of which grew significantly at the time of economic prosperity, in the years of plenty. It fell rapidly in periods of calamity : dearth, plague, etc. In the entire period under study, the real-estate value – depending on methods of analysis used – decreased about 15 %, despite generally favourable economic trends and a significant rise in grain prices. The reaction of the landowners is noteworthy : the rate of land alienation transactions fell even lower by at least 30 %.

It is also interesting to note that the indebted real-estates retained the stability of the nominal price for a considerable time. After the debt was paid off, the estate again was subjected to the market mechanisms. Similarly, the prices in interfamilial transactions were 'frozen', which reflected the protectionist estate policy of the family toward its own kin. In both cases, the prices – repeated in numerous deeds – greatly differed from the real value of land.

The pattern of individual and group behaviour of the Kalisz gentry on their local real-estate market displays the economic passivity of the landowners. The gentry land market viewed from the perspective of perpetual alienation of land was the zone of mainly defensive activity. Much more effort was put into retaining or keeping the estate than in the activities centred on expansion. No competitive areas of profit making accessible to Polish gentry led to focusing their attention on defending the estate's status. In Polish conditions, land was the only real and most important source of the gentry's social status. Paradoxically it was more difficult to stay on top in case of the ill-differentiated social and wealth community of Kalisz County. There was no severe competition between the rich and the poor. The struggle for land and its profits concerned mostly equals coming from the same social milieu. Equal chances and similar possibilities of action meant for most equal hopes and equal dangers.

MODERN PERIOD

INTERNATIONAL COOPERATION AND DOMESTIC CARTEL CONTROL: THE INTERNATIONAL STEEL CARTEL, 1926-1938

DANIEL BARBEZAT

The conclusion of the First World War marked the end of the economic and political environment that had developed over the course of the 19th century. During the years 1919 through 1939 Western European nations had to redefine themselves and their strained economic relationships. This whole adjustment process was carried out by an intricate set of international agreements and organizations, which attempted to restore order to the chaotic face of Europe. The emphasis on the new international order did not eliminate the passionate nationalism of the late 19th century, far from it. The international agreements were made with a keen eye to preserve and extend the political and economic power of their constituent countries.

One of the most important commercial agreements during this period was the International Steel Cartel (ISC), with founding members Germany, France, Belgium and Luxemburg. In their attempt to reorganize their steel markets during the 1920s and 1930s, these countries used complicated cartel arrangements that were forced to change with the shocks of the period. My dissertation is a description and analysis of these cartel arrangements and their modifications through time. Rather than treating the ISC as a single entity with its own policies and targets, I examine the cartel members and how they interacted in the context of this international agreement. In addition, special attention is paid to the different cartelized products and their markets. In this way, features of the cartel and its markets are understood as special features relating to one or more of the members, and I am then able to compare inter-member gains and losses in terms of their individual aims. This methodology provides new insights into the behaviour of international organizations and is a fruitful way of attempting to understand cooperative behaviour. Had economists looked to the structure of the members of the O.P.E.C. cartel and the product they controlled, they would have better been able to predict its impact over the 1970s.

By looking at the internal structures of the cartel's members and their respective economic environments, I conclude that the international agreements changed as was needed, given the conditions of the domestic and international markets. Over the 1920s the cartel structure was simple, yet by limiting trade between the major steel producers, it successfully provided the foundation upon which the countries could reorganize and operate their own domestic cartels. The cartel was organized around fixed total steel production shares; prices were not set by the cartel. Each member had a given production share of the total cartel production and was penalized for over-quota production. In addition to the production shares, the member groups agreed to limit trade between them. These import restrictions gave the domestic cartels monopoly power and enabled them to price in excess of the world price plus the tariff.

Germany thrived in this environment and expanded production and trade throughout the decade; she was able also to profit from her highly vertically and horizontally concentrated industry and create a strong system of internal cartels. In addition to good domestic conditions for their cartel development, the Germans had the trade restriction agreements of the international agreements which protected Germany from low-price French and Belgian semi-finished products, allowing the German firms to exploit their domestic market power. However, Germany was often over its production quota and had to pay large penalties. I show that the net penalties were lower than previously estimated and that the growth of German penalties was not only due to expanding German demand; after 1927 the Germany had an export quota. The growth of German exports increased the German penalties significantly because over-quota export penalties were four times as much per ton as over-quota total production.

The other countries required the 1920s just to regroup, and it was not until after 1930 that France and Belgium were ready to attempt global domestic policies for steel production and sales. Both of these countries, however, were plagued by their non-integrated steel works (re-rollers), which were continual problems for their domestic cartels. The re-rollers required steel ingots as inputs and therefore resented policies aimed at increasing steel prices. They were the source of endless coordination problems for both France and Belgium and go a long way in explaining the difficulty in forming their domestic cartels. The problem was further complicated by French firms selling allied Belgian re-rollers their steel inputs. This weakened Belgian internal control over the re-rollers, so that the re-rollers could remain cartel outsiders and disrupt Belgian cartel policies.

The operation of the international cartel during the 1920s reflected these differences between the national groups. Using a market-share response model and calculating correlations of changes in market shares, I show that the countries with the most similar internal organizations, France, Belgium and Luxemburg, were the most coordinated in their production and had a rival relationship with the German group, which had its own internal agenda created by its domestic cartels. These relationships held until 1930 when the French steel industry organized their nationally united steel cartel agreement, headed by the *Comptoir Sidérurgique de la France.* With the French industrial organization becoming different from the Belgian and Luxemburger organizations, the cartel production coordination between the countries broke down. The onset of the European depression saw an increasingly rivalrous steel industry and a abrogation of the cartel agreements of the 1920s.

Although the Germans prospered in the late 1920s, they were hit most severely by the world depression. This was mainly because their rigid internal structures did not allow them the needed elasticity to adapt to the new market conditions. As a graphic example of this, I outline the impact of the internal agreement between the German steel producers and steel finishers, represented by the *Arbeitgemeinschaft der verarbeitenen Industrie (AVI).* The AVI agreement linked domestic prices to world prices, by allowing domestic steel finishers the world prices for steel inputs for finished product destined to export markets; it operated well in the relatively stable 1920s but was an extreme burden when the world prices dropped after 1930. The French took this opportunity to profit from the Germans' misfortune and expanded output, while creating their own internal cartels which operated for the rest of the decade. Not only did the shock of the depression break the international cartel, it also marked a continued change in the relationship of the French group with the other national groups. As the French group began to conduct its own internal policies, it became less and less integrated with the Belgian and Luxemburg groups although it continued to have a rivalrous relationship with the German group. With the near collapse of the international market, the Belgian and Luxemburg groups clung together even more closely and acted as if they were a single unit.

After the shock of the depression, the national groups were ready again to reform their international agreements under the new conditions of their own internal organizations and the changes in the international markets. In the 1930s the Belgian steel industry, although never fully united behind a single organization, formed the *Comptoir de Vente Sidérurgique de la Belgique.* This organization governed all the domestic Belgian steel cartels and interacted with the newly formed international export cartel. The formation and operation of the Belgian cartels was a long and difficult process, and the plurality among steel producers made any universal policy almost impossible. Even though the cartels were fraught with difficulty, I show that the Belgian firms were able to receive prices in excess of marginal cost up until 1937. With the Belgian devaluation and the turmoil of the coming war, the Belgian firms were in disarray after 1937.

The French steel industry had similar problems in operating its cartels over the 1930s; although the French organizations were more complex than their Belgian counterparts, it is not clear that the French firms respected the cartels' rules. The French domestic cartels did manage, however, to coordinate the pricing of important steel merchants, bring the re-rollers somewhat under control and allow the French firms to participate in the international steel agreements. As in the Belgian case, the increasing British tariffs hurt the French industry and the French were forced to reorganize after 1935 when the British Steel Federation was finally integrated into the international agreements. I conclude that the French cartels were largely unsuccessful in allowing the French firms to receive high prices (relative to their prime costs), especially after 1936 when the 40 hour law was applied and the Franc was sharply devalued.

As previously mentioned, the German steel industry was highly organized with single-product cartels for every major product. Even though the Germans were constrained by the international environment, the German steel industry did have a history of strong cartels and was situated in a very stable and growing domestic economy, something neither Belgium nor France had during the 1930s. Again using a Lerner monopoly power index, I show that the German firms were able to keep their prices higher than competitive prices. However, these powerful domestic cartels met with an even more powerful force – the Nationalist Socialist Party. Even though the Nazis supported some of the industrialists labor policy opinions, I found that the Nazi influence after 1936 became significantly more constraining the steel producers' pricing, selling and input purchasing policies. The strict exchange controls limited important Swedish ore imports and made other needed imports scarcer and therefore more expensive. In addition to the changes in commercial policy, the Nazis forced producers to include the smallest merchants into the domestic cartel agreements and not to price discriminate against them. So while the German steel producers had been able to handle their industrial problems, they were met with new constraints from the Nazi government.

All these domestic changes occurred in the context of a rich and complex international market for steel. The new international cartel, that was created in 1933, regulated exports rather than total production, with a number of single product cartels, allocating quotas and also setting prices for different export markets. This new arrangement continued to protect the domestic markets of each of the member countries, permitting them to continue the formation and operation of their domestic cartels. The domestic and international cartels had a distinct symbiotic relationship; it was only with the proper organization of the domestic steel industries that the different national groups could work with each other, yet it was only through international accords that the domestic firms received the necessary protection to coordinate domestic policy.

Although the historiography of the international cartels is very negative about their economic impact, I find that the international export cartels were successful in organizing the major steel customers, so that the member nations could effectively price discriminate across different markets with different price elasticities. The cartel did this through the establishment of exclusive sales organizations in importing countries. This guaranteed that the products would not be resold in the world market and allowed the firms to receive prices over the 'world price'. Using regressions to estimate exports, I show that the international cartel members were responsive to their export quotas and did seem to adjust sales so that they would be at their quota allowances. I find also that the national groups did seem to use exports as a 'safety-valve', yet the groups did respond to their over or under quota positions.

The story that emerges from my dissertation is that the form of the international cooperation in each period was directly linked to both the nature of the product controlled and, most importantly, the environment in which members of the various national groups found themselves. Overall, I conclude that although the various cartels were not operating as we would expect, they were successful in reestablishing a coordinated European steel market and providing a structure in which the steel firms in the member groups could benefit.

BRITISH TECHNOLOGY AND NORWEGIAN INDUSTRIALIZATION: THE DIFFUSION OF TEXTILE TECHNIQUES FROM 1845 TO 1870

KRISTINE BRULAND

Underlying this thesis is the idea that we still know relatively little about the technological basis of European industrialization in the mid-nineteenth century. In many countries growth either began or accelerated from the 1840s, with higher rates of fixed capital formation and greater use of modern technologies. Most of the historiography of European industrialization concentrates on the social, cultural and economic preconditions of this growth – following the pioneering contribution of Alexander Gerschenkron – rather than addressing the more direct question of how it actually occurred or was possible at the level of plants and enterprises. The latter problem is explored in this thesis, which analyses the technological basis of growth and change in Norwegian cotton and woollen entreprises after 1845. In particular, the role of the diffusion or transfer of technologies from Britain, and the agencies through which that diffusion was channeled, are described and assessed.

For what might be called the 'early phase' of European industrialization, to about 1830, we know the importance of the diffusion of technologies and skills from Britain. A number of writers have shown the key role played by British engineers, entrepreneurs, skilled workers and so on in spreading the skills associated with what Pollard calls 'the new technology'. Although machinery exports were prohibited, equipment and information did flow abroad, through smuggling, through industrial espionage, through technical societies and numerous other channels. What effect did the removal of the prohibitions on the export of machinery, in 1843, have on this flow of men, information and equipment? A core idea of this thesis is that this liberalizing measure must be seen in the context of the development of the UK capital goods industry at that time.

Capital goods production, in the form of iron and steel, power sources, and so on, had been a key component of the industrial revolution. But in the period to 1840 the increasing mechanisation of production led to the emergence of specialized machine-making firms, a mechanical engineering industry which produced machines and equipment for final-output-producing industries. This was a development of considerable significance, for it shifted the burden of generating process innovations away from machinery-using firms onto specialized producers. By 1841 there were 115 such firms in Lancashire alone, with a capital of over £ 1.5 million, and employing over 17,000 workers. The bulk of these firms were textile engineers, producing the whole range of machines and equipment necessary for modern textile production. Allowing these firms freely to export their products may well have substantially affected the pace and scope of European industrialization, by opening up to emergent or potential European entrepreneurs the possibility of matching the technical level of British production. Whether this happened, however, and how it happened, is a matter of examining industrial development at the level of individual firms, looking at the precise character of the contacts they had and transactions they made with British textile engineering firms. It is that task which occupies the bulk of the empirical sections of this thesis.

This thesis, is, therefore, an examination of the diffusion of British textile technologies from Britain to Norway through the activities of firms within the UK textile engineering sector. The focus is not on the Norwegian industry as a whole, but on six firms within it, with a primary emphasis on one firm, the Hjula Weavery (which was in fact a large integrated spinning and weaving establishment, working in both cotton and wool). The empirical study consists of the following:

(1) An examination of the changing fixed capital stocks of 10 firms within the Norwegian industry. This is based on fire insurance records of the *Brankassa,* the state fire insurance company, which list, at frequent intervals, stocks of power equipment and textile machinery. In general, fixed capital stock of these firms rose rapidly from the mid-1840s, indicating a substantial programme of equipment acquisition. These fixed capital stocks are then disaggregated into stocks of 'direct production equipment': preparatory and finishing equipment, spinning machinery, and weaving machinery. Then, through an

examination of invoice records, it is shown that this buildup of equipment was based on acquisition from Britain : of 345 items of machinery acquired by two firms over a fifteen year period, 343 originated in Britain. There was, therefore, a substantial process of technology transfer or diffusion. Subsequent parts of the study examine details of how this occurred.

(2) Technology transfer requires the flow of general technical information on the broad range and structure of technical developments abroad, and on the availability of equipment. Two channels of such flow are described for Norway : firstly, the activities of technical societies, which through programmes of meetings and exhibitions, and regular publication of journals, communicated a wide range of information on British technological developments. Most of the major Norwegian textile entrepreneurs belonged to one or more of these societies. Secondly, there was foreign travel, specifically to Britain, on the part of textile entrepreneurs. This travel, which in some cases included periods of training in British textile mills, was frequent and extensive, and clearly very much a part of the diffusion process.

(3) The UK textile engineering sector was central to technology transfer from Britain. Through an examination of correspondence files, invoices, diaries, and other firm records, a picture is constructed of the general activities of UK firms in the Norwegian textile sector. Over 330 UK firms of all types had some sort of contact with the Norwegian firms studies here; of these, 84 were textile engineers. These firms keenly sought sales in the Norwegian market, and were prepared to provide a wide range of what might be called 'ancillary services' with the equipment they sold. Essentially these firms provided as well as all types of machinery and associated inputs, the following services :

(i) Information relating to the technical aspects of setting up textile enterprises; on the assessment and evaluation of new machines and equipment; on the availability of equipment types; and on the choice of technique.

(ii) Information on the construction, setting-up and operation of techniques, including diagrams and drawings, and including also information on prices and costs of production.

(iii) Information on types of output, and on levels of output to be expected with particular machines.

(iv) The supply of labour : UK textile engineers frequently

advertised for, interviewed, and recruited all types of skilled labour and supervisory staffs for Norwegian firms. This included arranging contracts and journeys, and often extended to making payments to the families in Britain of UK workers in Norway.

The conclusion which emerges from this is that UK textile engineers were prepared to do a great deal more than simply sell machines. They were, in effect, frequently selling 'packages' of technology which included a complex array of information, equipment and labour, and they were prepared to offer advice and assistance on a continuing basis.

(4) In their dealings with UK textile engineers, Norwegian firms also made use of a heterogeneous collection of agents. These were sometimes specialists, who placed a detailed knowledge of particular parts of the textile engineering industry at the service of their Norwegian customers. Others were active in some other part of the complex of textile activities: some were raw material suppliers, some were chemists (selling dyestuffs), some were dealers in second-hand parts and equipment, some were finance houses (whose activities merged into merchant banking), some were agents active in general trade with Scandinavia (in, e.g., cotton manufactures, timber and so on). Such firms were frequently ready to expand their activities into dealing with textile engineers, into seeking out particular machines and equipment, and into general technical problem-solving on behalf of Norwegian firms. 26 such firms are identified, performing a range of functions similar to those of UK textiles engineers themselves.

(5) Norwegian textile development was accompanied by an inflow of skilled labour and managerial expertise from Britain. Among the firms studied here, a total of 96 British workers can be traced to 1870, 20 of them women. Broadly speaking, these workers fall into three categories: (1) fitters and mechanics, who set up equipment; (2) skilled operatives of various kinds; (3) managerial and supervisory staff. Much of the inflow was organized through British textile engineers and agents, but in turn these workers and managers performed important technical functions. The functions included the provision of specific skill inputs; a wide range of technical information and advice; assistance and guidance in contacts with British firms; skill transmission (i.e. instruction and training of Norwegian workers,

and indeed of entrepreneurs); and supervision and management. British managers and supervisors from time to time advised on the employment of UK workers, advised on prices and suitability of equipment, on specifications of new equipment and so on. They also travelled to Britain on behalf of their Norwegian employers to order equipment and parts. In general, this labour inflow appears to have been a central component of the overall process of diffusion.

(6) Finally, there is a discussion of the way in which interrelationships among Norwegian firms operated to diffuse the new technology.

The central theme of this thesis is the importance of active market-seeking by UK textile engineers in the development of the Norwegian textile industry. Norwegian textile entrepreneurs were, in a technological sense, usually inexperienced and lacking technical expertise; this potential obstacle to diffusion was overcome by the willingness of UK machinery suppliers and agents to provide not only equipment but a wide range of technical services. If this experience is at all typical – as a concluding section argues it may be – then although this thesis has a very narrow focus, it may contribute to a new perspective on European industrialization. That industrialization may not have been either an imitation of or a departure from the British model, but in some industries a tangible extension of it, an organic development out of its British predecessor, with the transmitting agent being the British capital goods industry in general, and mechanical and textile engineering industries in particular.

FARMERS AS ENTREPRENEURS: REGULATION AND INNOVATION IN AMERICAN AGRICULTURE DURING THE TWENTIETH CENTURY

SALLY CLARKE

In 1933, as part of President Franklin D. Roosevelt's New Deal, the federal government introduced three types of farm regulation: first, a voluntary system of production controls, based on acreage restrictions; second, a system of price controls; and third, a public system for providing short- and long-term credit. What is striking about the regulation is that its introduction in the 1930s coincided with the start of a so-called 'revolution' in agricultural productivity: in the three decades years prior to 1930, total factor productivity in the farm sector increased at a mere 0.5 % annual rate. By contrast, between 1935 and 1975, total factor productivity in farming increased at a 3 % annual rate – a performance that surpassed rates achieved in all but two industries of the manufacturing sector. Even more striking were farmers' gains in labour productivity. Whereas prior to 1930 farmers managed less than a 1 % annual rate of growth of labour productivity, after 1935 gains in labour productivity averaged more than 4.5 % per year. Indeed, by 1980 one farmer fed 76 Americans, on average, or 8 times the number fed in 1930 (Kendrick, 1961, p. 366; Mansfield, 1980, p. 565; and U.S. Department of Agriculture, 1982, p. 63).

My purpose in this dissertation is to assess the role that government regulation played in farmers' productivity revolution. In recent years, Americans have become increasingly disenchanted with regulation. Taking a short-term perspective, critics frequently charge that regulation reduces efficiency because government controls fix prices above or below levels that would prevail in a free market. In my own study, I take exception with this negative perspective. Rather than focus on short-term changes in prices, I ask how regulation affected farmers' long-term investment calculus. In particular, I test the proposition that regulation actually accelerated the rate of productivity growth because it mitigated certain risks inherent in farmers' commodity markets so as to create a new climate for investment. My analysis is divided into two parts : in the first part, I examine how regulation changed farmers' investment markets and encouraged higher rates of productivity growth; in the second part, I consider the consequences of government intervention for the farm sector as a whole in the decades after the Great Depression.

I begin the first part of this study with the notion that New Deal regulation may not have contributed to farmers' revolution in productivity. It is possible to argue, for instance, that in the years prior to 1930 farmers attained few gains in productivity simply because researchers had not introduced productivity-enhancing technology. Alternatively, it may be argued that, even if the technology was available and if farmers had encountered barriers to investment prior to 1930, regulation failed to remove the risks to farm investment. The importance of regulation, then, hinges on answers to three questions : First, did farmers hesitate to adopt technology prior to the introduction of regulation? Second, if farmers shunned technology, what problems did they confront? Third, did regulation remove farmers' investment problems?

I assess these questions in a detailed study of one region in the United States, the Corn Belt, in the years immediately before and after regulation took effect (approximately from 1920 to 1940. I chose to study the Corn Belt for two reasons. First, the Corn Belt is one of the largest farm regions in the United States; it includes parts of many states, of which the five most important are Illinois, Indiana, Iowa, Missouri, and Ohio. Second, the Corn Belt was one region in which three important inventions were introduced during the interwar years : the tractor, the mechanical corn picker, and hybrid corn. Of the three inventions, the tractor was the most important. It was introduced during the 1920s, whereas the other two inventions were introduced during the 1930s. Thus, the tractor allows me to answer the first question – namely, whether prior to the coming of regulation farmers were reluctant to invest in new technology despite their intensely competitive markets.

The experience of the tractor indicated that during the 1920s farmers had delayed investments. I estimate, based simply on the tractor's cost savings relative to that of a team of horses, that more than half of all farmers in the Corn Belt could have reduced their cost of production by adopting the mechanical invention. In reality, however, only a quarter of the farmers made investments.

This conservative behaviour is important because it translated into fewer gains in labour productivity. During the 1920s, the tractor accounted for nearly all gains in labour productivity. I calculate that if those farmers who could have reduced costs by investing in a tractor had done so, then labour productivity would have risen by 12 % for the decade rather than the actual increase of 8 % (Works Progress Administration, 1938; and Reynoldson, 1933, p. 22). In other words, gains in labour productivity in the Corn Belt would have been 50 % higher had farmers based investments simply on cost savings.

Farmers delayed investments, I find, because technology presented a conflict for them between safety and productivity. Farmers' concern for safety arose out of the unstable nature of commodity markets. Because prices were volatile, farmers faced the risk that in any random year prices could fall below their average cost of production – turning profits into losses. To contain the risk of ruinous prices, farmers developed a simple strategy: they relied on resources they never paid for in cash but instead obtained from their farms. Farmers could opt for this strategy because they rarely paid cash for their two most important items – labour and horses. Farmers obtained labour from themselves and their families. Similarly, horses were raised, fed, and pastured on the farm itself. As farmers avoided actual cash expenses, they reduced the risk that, even if prices fell sharply, they would actually lose money.

In this way, farmers obtained greater security, but their safety strategy nevertheless had its own price, or penalty. The strategy implicitly made farmers judge technology on the basis of an invention's cash demands rather than on the basis of an invention's efficiency. For some inventions, like hybrid seed, farmers paid small sums of cash each year. These inventions therefore exerted modest increases in cash budgets and imposed a modest financial risk. Machines, however, such as tractors and harvesters, were often very expensive, and they forced farmers to elect between safety and productivity. Insofar as farmers chose safety, they slowed the rate of diffusion and slowed the rate of productivity growth.

The tractor illustrates the financial risks that farmers confronted. The machine consumed $ 350 in cash each year for fixed and operating charges. Or put another way, the tractor required an average 25 % increase in farmers' cash budgets from $ 1,400 to $ 1,750. In a quantitative study of farmers in Illinois and Iowa counties, I assess the effect of the tractor's cash demands on the pace of the machine's diffusion. The analysis indicated that in counties where the tractor imposed a relatively larger percentage increase in cash expenses, proportionately more farmers put off investments. Indeed, the rate of diffusion of the tractor was closely associated with the machine's relative financial burden. By placing safety ahead of productivity, then, farmers often delayed investments and slowed the rate of productivity growth.

By the 1930s, this investment dilemma was compounded by a second problem : debts many farmers had acquired during World War I. For those farmers who had mortgaged their land, and roughly 40 % had done so, interest payments might consume what cash was available to purchase expensive equipment. Moreover, after the Crash of 1929, payments became extraordinarily burdensome. Not only did debts preclude new investments, but they also ruined thousands of farmers. In 1932 and again in 1933, close to 8 % of indebted farmers in the Midwest declared bankruptcy (Stauber and Regan, 1935, p. 30).

In 1933, with the hope of ending the farm crisis, New Deal politicians created three regulatory agencies : the Agricultural Adjustment Administration, the Commodity Credit Corporation, and the Farm Credit Administration. The agencies were instructed to shore up prices and to reduce the burden of farm debts. Yet, in carrying out these relief missions, I argue that two regulatory agencies also resolved much of farmers' conflict between safety and productivity. The first agency, the Commodity Credit Corporation (CCC), dealt with the financial conflict posed by expensive technology, like the tractor. The Commodity Credit Corporation was created in the fall of 1933. Fearing that farmers would not have enough money to see them through the coming months, the CCC was designed to put cash into farmers' pockets immediately. The agency operated as follows : farmers borrowed a sum of cash equal to the amount of corn put up as collateral times a fixed price per bushel. This fixed price, or loan rate as it was known, acted as a minimum price. If the CCC set the loan rate high enough, then it would guarantee farmers their cost of production on a *cash* basis. Indeed, this is what happened. During the 1930s, the CCC set its minimum price at a level that guaranteed farmers 85 to 95 % of their cost of production where all costs (land, labour, and horses included) were assessed at their cash or market value. Because the CCC guaranteed the average cost of production, farmers no longer needed to choose technology that conserved cash. Instead, farmers were free to choose technology simply on the basis of its efficiency.

While the Commodity Credit Corporation removed much of the risk posed by expensive technology, the second agency, the Farm Credit Administration (FCA), reduced the burden of debts. Between 1933 and 1936, the FCA offered a series of emergency loans intended to shrink the size of debts, cut interest rates, and extend the terms of loans. These FCA loans, along with refinancing efforts of private lenders, served to cut the burden of interest payments from more than 9 % of farmers' cash income in 1929 to less than 5 % after 1935 (Horton, 1942, p. 32; and Farm Credit Administration, 1936, p. 7).

By the second half of the 1930's, then, the New Deal regulatory agencies had created a new climate for farm investment. Farmers, no longer threatened by unstable prices or burdened by large debts, responded by investing in the productivity-enhancing technology. Tractor sales recovered from their depressed years of 1932 and 1933; indeed, from 1936 to 1939, tractor sales averaged 25 % higher than sales in 1929, the best year prior to the depression (Brodell and Pike, 1942, p. 2). Moreover, as farmers bought tractors they substantially closed the gap between the rate of investment predicted simply by cost savings and their actual rate of investment. That is, as of 1939, roughly 60 % of farmers in Illinois and Iowa should have invested in tractors simply on the basis of cost savings, and between 50 and 60 % had done so.

Aside from the tractor, midwestern farmers also invested in the other two inventions – hybrid corn and the mechanical corn picker. Hybrid corn offered roughly a 200 % return on investment with little risk of actually losing money. The seed was introduced in the mid-1930s, and by the end of the decade farmers had planted it in nearly two-thirds of all corn fields. In the case of hybrid corn, I conclude that farmers invested in the seed because it was so cheap; regulation most likely played little role in the seed's rapid diffusion. As to the mechanical corn picker, it is impossible to determine whether regulation caused farmers to invest in this invention because the machine became profitable in the mid-1930s, that is, at the same time that the regulatory programs were introduced. Still, it is also possible that farmers could have clung to their conservative strategy, ignoring the safer investment climate and delaying investments. But this did not happen. Within three years after the mechanical corn picker became profitable, roughly three-fourths of farmers who should have used it did so. Overall, during the Great Depression, farmers in the Corn Belt doubled their rate of growth of labour productivity set in the 1920s. I estimate that regulation was associated with perhaps one-third of one-half the gains.

In the second part of the dissertation, I examine the effects of regulation for the farm sector as a whole in the period since 1930. Legislators originally designed the Commodity Credit Corporation to prevent prices from falling, and assumed that in the event that prices met the intended goal, that is, if prices rose, the agency would play no role. This policy, while intended to counter low prices in the Great Depression, had ironic results when it was employed after World War II. From 1946 to 1970, as increases in supply pushed prices lower, the CCC placed strong supports under prices. The agency not only stabilized prices, but it also subsidized farm income and farm investment. Moreover, as regulation stimulated higher rates of investment, it accelerated gains in productivity, and by implication, accelerated the decline in the number of farms. Regulation, however, had much different consequences when in the 1970s the demand for cash crops, such as corn, cotton, and wheat, sent prices to high levels. With this new prosperity, the CCC was instructed not to raise its loan rate. Thus, once demand subsided, the CCC was unable to slow the drop in prices. I conclude that for several decades regulation had stimulated extraordinarily high rates of investment, only to leave farmers vulnerable to a credit crisis in the 1980s.

REFERENCES

A.P. Brodell and R.S. Pike, *Farm Tractors: Type, Size, Age, and Life* (Washington, D.C.: U.S. Bureau of Agricultural Economics, FM 30, 1942).

Farm Credit Administration, *Third Annual Report of the Farm Credit Administration* (Washington, D.C. : U.S. Government Printing Office, 1936).

D.C. Horton, H.C. Larson, and N.J. Wall, *Farm-Mortgage Credit Facilities in the United States,* U.S. Department of Agriculture Miscellaneous Publication 478 (1942).

J.W. Kendrick, *Productivity Trends in the United States* (Princeton, 1961).

E. Mansfield, 'Technology and Productivity in the United States', M. Feldstein, ed., *The American Economy in Transition* (Chicago, 1980), 563-596.

L.A. Reynoldson, W.R. Humphries, S.R. Speelman, E.W. McComas, and W.H. Youngman, *Utilization and Cost of Power on Corn Belt Farms,* U.S. Department of Agricultural Technical Bulletin 384 (October 1933).

S.R. Stauber and M.M. Regan, *The Farm Real Estate Situation, 1933-1934,* U.S. Department of Agriculture Circular 354 (April 1935).

U.S. Department of Agriculture, *Economic Indicators of the Farm Sector : Production and Efficiency Statistics, 1980,* Statistical Bulletin 679 (January 1982).

Works Progress Administration, *Changes in Technology and Labor Requirements in Production : Corn,* National Research Project Report No. A-5 (Philadelphia, 1938).

THE EVOLUTION OF QUEBEC GOVERNMENT SPENDING, 1867-1969

RUTH DUPRÉ

There seems to be a tradition in Canada of considering the province of Quebec with its French-speaking and Catholic majority as rather singular and one of the peculiarities most often stressed is the historial behaviour of its government. It is widely believed (Marr and Paterson, for instance, 1980, p. 445) that Quebec did not have an interventionist government, contrarily to the other Canadian provinces and indeed to most Western countries, before the 1960s. This thesis wants to determine whether this was the case by analyzing Quebec government spending in the period from 1867, the year of the Confederation to 1969, the end of the 'Quiet Revolution'. Spending is of course only one of the instruments governments use. Regulation, public ownership, and more recently tax expenditures, are also important but they cannot be quantified and their evolution over time cannot be readily observed. In what follows, the main findings are outlined under three headings corresponding to the three objectives of the thesis : the building of a consistent fiscal series, the formulation and estimation of a model to try to explain the evolution of the expenditures, and the comparison with Ontario to verify Quebec's uniqueness.

A CENTURY OF PUBLIC FINANCES IN QUEBEC

The primary source of fiscal data, the Public Accounts, are kept primarily to ensure the 'accountability' of public spending and do not generally provide convenient information. A few examples should suffice to show that they cannot be taken at face value. The data are classified by ministry or department but this is not a very useful breakdown as some government functions are carried on by several departments, some departments are spending on different functions and the government structure is frequently modified. Secondly, as late as 1953, various revenues were netted out of expenditures, a procedure applied very often but not always with the result that total expenditure and revenue are inconsistent over time. These totals are indeed very difficult to interpret, especially before the 1930s, as they included all kinds of outlays – capital, extraordinary, trust funds, debt repayments – not clearly identified.

It is however possible to correct these problems using the incredible amount of details the Public Accounts contain to derive some consistent series. We build annual series, global and disaggregated, of expenditure and revenue from 1867 to 1969. Both are broken down in large categories – ten for expenditures and four for revenues – and each category is further disaggregated: for instance in education, we have information on how much was spent for universities, technical schools, agricultural schools, primary education, libraries, and the like.

In 1969, the Quebec government expenditure size and pattern are beyond recognition from a century earlier. Expenditures which amounted to a little over $ 1 million in 1867, total more than $ 3 billions in 1969, thus multiplied by 3.000. As prices and population increase by about 400 % in the same period, real expenditures per capita are multiplied by 100. Their composition radically changed: while law and order represented almost half of the budget and social spending less than a quarter in 1870, their respective proportions are 8 and 60 % a century later. Let us sketch very briefly how it happened.

At the time of Confederation, the predominant view about the role of the State is that 'the government governs best which governs least'. The provincial governments of the new Dominion of Canada are even more limited as the central government takes over the most important functions of the time – defence, economic development and interprovincial transportation – leaving to them local matters such as education, justice, health, then considered as minor responsibilities. This will not impede the Quebec government to catch the railway fever and to spend the enormous sum of $ 26 millions in aid to railways between 1873 and 1900 with dramatic consequences on the public finances of the province. This is only in 1912 that the government will get involved again in a large project with the Good Roads Act. At the eve of the First World War, the Quebec government is still very much a '19th century government' whose priority goes to transportation and law and order.

The year 1921 marks the beginning in Quebec of the intervention of the state in social welfare with the Public Charities Act under which the provincial government, the municipalities and the private charitable institutions share the costs of caring for the needy in institutions. During the Great Depression of the 1930s, the very severe unemployment problem asks for exceptional measures. The initiative comes from the federal government which sets up in 1930 the Unemployment Aid Act, a joint federal provincial program of direct relief and public work subsidies. In addition to these emergency measures, the Quebec government finally adopts the federal-provincial old age pension program in 1936 and a pension scheme to needy mothers and blind people in 1939. Welfare expenditures which had always been less than 15 % of the budget, represent in the thirties more than half.

During the Second World War, as in the First, public expenditure and taxation are concentrated at the central government level. Quebec government spending does not grow from 1940 to 1944 but important regulations are introduced in various spheres : the vote to women in 1940, compulsory education in 1943, and the nationalization of the 'Montreal Light, Heat & Power' and the 'Beauharnois Power' to form Hydro-Quebec in 1944.

In the same year, Duplessis, who was to retain his office until his death in 1959, and its Union Nationiale party end the long fifty-year reign (1896-1944 briefly interrupted by Duplessis first mandate in 1936-9). The conventional wisdom in Canadian historiography (McRoberts and Postgate, 1983, pp. 79-83, 96-97) is that Duplessis was extremely conservative, ideologically and financially. This must be indeed where the idea of a historically non-interventionist state comes from. On one hand, our data support the view of a Duplessis government living 'within its means' as expenditures and revenues are moving very closely and there are more years with a surplus than with a deficit. However, they do not support the contention that the structure of spending remains traditional and that the welfare state does not gain ground in Quebec before the 1960s. Under Duplessis, spending on education, health and welfare account for 40 to 50 % of the total while outlays on law and order are less than 10 %.

The final decade of our study is the most notorious of all in Quebec with respect to government intervention. The term 'Quiet

Revolution' has been coined by reporters to describe the transformation of the role of the state. Lesage Liberal government's (1960-5) most important actions are concentrated in three fields: natural resources with the nationalization of electricity in 1962, health with the hospitalization insurance and education with the creation of the Ministry of Education and free universal secondary education. There is undoubtedly an impressive growth in government expenditures in this decade as they increase by 400 % and by 260 % in real terms. The trend towards social spending depicted in the Duplessis period is not only maintained but is accentued as education, health and welfare come to represent two thirds of the budget at the end of the decade. This is not however a phenomenon unique to Quebec. For instance, Ontario had very similar rates of growth. Indeed, this was the case in the rest of Canada and in most OECD countries. What is unique to Quebec are the institutional changes resulting from the 'crowding out' of the Catholic Church and of the federal government by the provincial government. In the fields of education, health and welfare, the Quebec government replaced financial assistance by control of most of the institutions until then in the hands of the Church. The Quebec government also became more assertive and opted out of several federal-provincial programs to set up its own public pension plan and medicare.

A MODEL OF GOVERNMENT BEHAVIOUR

Utility maximization under constraint is widely used by economists to characterize government decision-making behaviour. There is however a particular difficulty in determining what exactly it is that governments maximize: the population's utility or their own? Following the Public Choice School, the government is assumed here to maximize its own utility. In its utility function, there are three arguments: expenditures, taxes, and borrowing. Some expenditures, such as roadbuilding, can be said to increase the government's utility because they may increase its probability of reelection while other outlays, such as education or justice, with no electoral virtue in the period we are concerned with, may give the government satisfaction for more subtle motives à la Breton (1974, p. 124): that is, 'personal power, image in history, pursuit of lofty personal ideals'. Both taxes and borrowing, as alternative means of financing expenditures, provide disutility.

From the maximization of this utility function under a budgetary constraint, five equations are derived for expenditures in education, health-welfare, agriculture, transportation, and all others. Each category is assumed to be affected by government revenues, derived from the budgetary constraint, and by provincial income, a variable reflecting demand as well as supply forces. Political preoccupations are introduced in the equations of agriculture and transportation, the two categories of spending historically electoralist. Additional variables specific to each category of expenditures are also included. For instance, the rate of urbanization and demographic variables, such as the proportion in the population of children and of old age persons, are considered as demand factors for social spending on education, health and welfare. On the supply side of these expenditures, the substitution between the public and private sector is especially interesting here because of the predominance of the Catholic Church in the social field for most of Quebec history. Unfortunately, no data on the Church spending are available but we use a proxy the proportion of religious in the total number of teachers in the education equation.

The estimation results give a mitigated, at the most, support to Wagner's Law, one of the classic hypothesis of the public finance literature. Our income coefficients are positive and statistically significant in only two of the five categories of expenditures: education and miscellaneous (which includes 'law and order'). The explanation varies with the category of spending. For welfare outlays, a falling rather than a rising provincial income may lead to an increase in the demand for government commitment as in the Great Depression of the 1930s. In the case of transportation, it is possible that, after the completion of the network, railway and later road outlays became less important regardless of provincial income. However, our attempt to take into account some institutional and political factors produces encouraging results as the Catholic Church proxy and the electoral variables are generally statistically significant.

A COMPARISON WITH ONTARIO

In order to challenge the conventional wisdom of a unique non-interventionist state in Quebec until the 1960s, the Quebec government spending pattern has to be compared. Ontario, the neighbouring province, is the most obvious candidate for the comparison. The two provinces are different in may respects : the ethnic composition of their population, their industrial structure, their macroeconomic and unemployment performance. But they share a common geography and, to a large extent, history, and a similar timing and pattern of industrialization and urbanization. There are indeed a large number of comparisons of Quebec-Ontario agriculture, industrialization, business cycles and government intervention. Moreover, some comparable data are available for almost the whole period as Drummond (1980) compiles Ontario fiscal series on the same basis as ours for 1867-1939 while Statistics Canada provincial public finance data begin in 1950.

The comparison shows some difference between the two provincial government spending patterns but not a systematically less interventionist government in Quebec as the conventional wisdom would have it. Quebec government outspends Ontario's almost until the First World War, mostly because of its heavier involvement in railway building in the last quarter of the nineteenth century. After the war, this pattern is reversed until the beginning of the 1960s when Quebec per capita public spending becomes once again larger than Ontario's. By the most conventional measure of government activity – the proportion of government spending in the GNP – Quebec is above Ontario throughout the whole period with the exception of 1920-35.

When one discusses the growth of government intervention in this century, it is often with the rise of the welfare state in mind. Provincial government expenditures on education, health and welfare show a strong upward trend in both provinces over the century since Confederation. While the growth rates are similar, the Quebec levels are systematically below Ontario's, which is not surprising given that the Catholic Church in Quebec assumed for a long time in these spheres, functions which were largely undertook by the state elsewhere. More surprising is that the gap considerably narrows and even disappears in the case of health and welfare at least from 1950 – perhaps before but we do not know as the Ontario data for the forties have not been compiled – casting some doubt on the uniqueness and revolutionary character of the decade of the sixties.

REFERENCES

A. Breton, *The Economic Theory of Representative Government* (Chicago, 1974).

I.M. Drummond, 'The Ontario "Exchequer", 1867-1940', unpublished paper (University of Toronto, 1980).

W. Marr and D. Paterson, *Canada: An Economic History* (Toronto, 1980).

K. McRoberts and D. Postgate, *Développement et modernisation du Québec* (Montreal, 1983).

Quebec, Province of, *Public Accounts,* annual (1868-1969).

Statistics Canada, *Financial Statistics of Provincial Governments,* 68-207, annual (Ottawa, 1950-1969).

SCIENCE AND TECHNOLOGY IN THE DEVELOPMENT OF THE GALICIAN OIL INDUSTRY

PIOTR FRANASZEK

Statistics on the world oil output in the latter part of the 19th century and the beginning of the 20th, before 1914, show an overwhelming domination by the United States. At the same time, there were three important producers of crude oil in Europe: Russia, Rumania, and Austro-Hungary, and specifically its northern province of Galicia. This was the southern part of Poland that had been annexed by Austria in 1772 in the partitioning of Poland by Russia, Prussia, and Austria.

Galicia was considerably less industrialized than the other regions of the Austro-Hungarian Monarchy. It has been said that profound social and economic backwardness was the outstanding feature of Galicia, and, in the latter part of the 19th century, the gap widened between the economic development of Galicia and that of the other parts of the country due to the development of rail transport. Eventually, since it produced agricultural products but had no domestic industry. Galicia became a large market for industrial goods. Galicia underwent its industrial revolution only in the beginning of the 20th century.

Unlike the rest of the pattern, Galician oil production was among the highest in the world. In 1909, Galicia ranked third in world oil production with a 5.1 % share (more than 2 million tons) behind the United States (61 %) and Russia (22 %).

What were the factors that caused the rapid emergence of this new production sector? Why did the Galician oil industry change from the protoindustrial stage to industrialization in such a relatively short time?

At the start of answering these questions, it should be noted that sources of oil, which had been known in Galicia for many years previously, conditioned the further development of oil extraction. In addition to these sources, however, there were other socio-economic factors that significantly influenced the Galician oil industry. The most important ones were the labour force, the outlet for Galician crude oil, capital, and the advances in the science and technology of oil production. These four factors, and other, less important ones, all shaped the Galician oil industry. Thus, we must determine their importance and identify the most significant of them.

The socio-economic structure of Galicia was characterized by a small number of landlords and an enormous number of smallholders and landless people. An agrarian reform in Galicia in 1848 increased social differentiation. As a result, the Galician oil industry from the outset witnessed a flow of unskilled labour from the agricultural sector. But this group could not become the motor for accelerating the process of oil production.

Shortage of capital was the next feature of the socio-economic backwardness of Galicia. The landowners had been indemnified by the State in 1848 but they wasted their funds on useless consumption. Those who did invest their money did it in agriculture or the food industry, particularly brewing and distilling, and a very few invested in the petroleum industry.

There was foreign capital, but it was not invested in the oil industry before large quantities of oil were believed to exist in Galicia. Foreign capital in significant amounts arrived in Galicia at the turn of the 19th century. This was largely German and English capital, and Austrian capital had been there for some time previously.

The Galician home market for crude oil was very weak. Although there were several dozen petroleum refineries in Galicia, their output of lighting kerosene was very small. Only about a quarter of Galician oil was distilled on the spot. Therefore, the huge Austrian and Hungarian refineries were the main outlet for Galician oil. Their monopolistic position determined the demand and the price.

The rapid expansion of Galician oil production and the evidence given above allow us to conclude that, to some extent, the Galician oil industry developed irrespective of the demand, an outlet, or sufficient capital. This means that the narrow and primarily socio-economic approach to the questions must be widened to include the impact of science and technology on Galician oil mining. Needless to say, this approach is more complex. We tested the hypothesis that the introduction of new techniques and innovations in oil drilling was of greater importance than the other factors in the development of the Galician oil industry.

The interaction between science and technology and Galician oil extraction began in the early 1860s with the application of the free-fall drilling method. Using this method, Robert Doms in Borysław and Henryk Walter in Bóbrka drilled the first oil wells in Galicia. The method spread little by little, particularly after steam engines were introduced in the mid-sixties.

Obviously, the introduction of the free-fall method was an important event. The system took the place of digging wells with shovels. Thanks to the free-fall method, oil production in Galicia increased more than tenfold from 2,182 tons in 1863 to 27,850 tons in 1883. But the system turned out to be effective only for shallow oil beds, which were soon exhausted. The system had to be improved. But, no sooner than when Albert Frauck tried to introduce some innovations, a new method, the so-called Canadian drilling system, came to Galicia. The introduction of the Canadian system marked a turning point in the history of the Galician oil industry.

The Canadian system was brought from Canada to Germany and then to Galicia by Bergheim and MacGarvey, a joint stock company, in the mid-1860s. The system soon replaced the free-fall method throughout the Galician oil fields. Its successful and rapid diffusion was possible because of the wooden construction of the Canadian rig. This was very important because industrially undeveloped Galicia was covered by large forests. In addition, the new system matched the local geological conditions.

At the beginning of the 20th century, thanks to the Canadian system, new oil-rich regions were discovered in East Galicia (Borysław, Drohobycz, Tustanowice). At the same time, the new system increased productivity of oil wells in West Galicia (Gorlice, Bóbrka, Jasło).

The application of the Canadian system enabled deep oil beds to be reached and increased the oil production in Galicia significantly :

Year	Production in tons
1886	43,104
1891	87,717
1896	262,356
1901	404,662
1906	737,194
1907	1,125,806
1908	1,718,030
1909	2,086,341
1910	1,766,017
1911	1,487,842
1914	655,614

The Canadian system was gradually improved in Galicia. The main changes concerned replacing labourious drilling rod bailing by rope bailing and the perfection of a driving system. Before long, the Canadian system was improved to the extent that it came to be called the Polish-Canadian drilling system. The most critical innovations were introduced by Wiliam MacGarvey, Wacław Wolski, Felicjan Lodziński, Leon Mikucki, and Władysław Włodarczyk.

The Canadian drilling system was used in Galicia until the end of the period we are concerned with here. The improved Canadian rigs allowed oil wells to be drilled with productivity that fully satisfied and even exceeded the oil demand in Galicia and Austria. The result was that three serious recessions occurred in Galicia in 1896, 1902, and 1909, when over production caused a sharp drop in the price of oil. Thus, as far as the economic development of the Galician oil industry was concerned, there was no need to introduce new mud-drilling methods that were being used elsewhere at the beginning of the 20th century. Nevertheless, it was in mud drilling that Galician scientific knowledge of oil drilling achieved its highest level.

Thanks to people like Albert Fauck, Wacław Wolski, Wiktor Petit, Leon Mikucki, Bonifacy Wiśniewski, Józef Howarth, and Wacław Pruszkowski, new, highley sophisticated mud-drilling rigs were built in Galicia. The international connections made these advances known in all the important oil countries of the period. They were appreciated everywhere they were used. Nevertheless, these rather expensive constructions could not be adopted in Galicia on a large scale, primarily because of the shortage of capital and, as noted above, the absence of a need for them. Therefore, the tests with new mud-drilling constructions were the effect of independent progress in science and technology in Galicia.

The people who introduced the significant innovations in the Galician oil industry were foreigners, who came to Galicia from the United States, Canada, or Germany, and Poles from Galicia and other parts of Poland. Most of them, being experienced businessmen and owners of oil companies, were highly skilled in the technical sciences. Their search for more efficient oil drilling methods was the result of their economic interests as well as their scientific research.

In addition to their role in the Galician economy and science, they contributed to the foundation of new technical schools and scientific societies related to the oil industry. Thanks to them, new books and technical journals of the oil industry were published. The same people aslo set out to establish a stable oil market. Striving to shake off the domination of Austro-Hungarian refineries over Galician oil, they formed an organization of Galician oil producers. Oil was sold only through the organization. At the beginning of the 20th century, the organization entered into negotiations with the American Standard Oil about supplying oil from Galicia. The talks were interrupted by the intervention of the Austrian government, which promised to build a new modern refinery in Galicia. In 1911, the refinery started operations in Drohobycz.

There is much evidence that the people engaged in the Galician oil industry combined several different elements of their activity.

In conclusion, it should be emphasized that strong links existed between science, technology and the oil industry in the latter half of the 19th century. This connection, which was quite obvious in many industrially advanced countries, had unique significance in Galicia. The independent progress of oil-drilling technology determined the short-lived marvel of the Galician oil industry, despite the socio-economic backwardness of the country.

THE AGRICULTURAL HISTORY OF THE FARMSTEAD OF SZÁNTÓDPUSZTA IN THE AGE OF CAPITALISM, 1848-1945

ÉVA MÁRIA FÜLÖP

THE BENEDICTINE ORDER IN HUNGARY

The Archabbey of Pannonhalma, centre of the newly reorganized Hungarian Benedictine congregation, was founded at the end of the Turkish occupation. The Benedictine monasteries of Bakonybél and Celldömölk were attached in 1636, the monastery of Tihany in 1716, and the monastery of Zalavár in 1888.

For the property of the abbey of Tihany, the Benedictine monastery of Altenburg in Austria paid the ransom for the war of liberation to the treasury in Vienna: 20,000 golden forints were paid in 1716 to Pannonhalma, because of the distance and the language problem.

The period from 1848 to 1945 was the period of the capitalist development of Hungarian agriculture, but elements of feudalism still survived as was the case elsewhere in Central Eastern Europe. We can divide this period into three parts: the first consists of the transition to capitalism after the emancipation of the serfs, the second the modernization with the introduction of capitalist agricultural techniques, and the third the attempt to meet the changing conditions between the two World Wars.

The land of the Archabbey of Pannonhalma and the other four monasteries of the Congregation amounted to about 60,000 cadastral yokes (1 yoke is a cadastral measure equaling about 0.76 hectares). This land was situated in the western part of the country in Transdanubia as a trust and was the economic base for maintaining the Archabbey, the four monasteries, two advanced schools (one for theology and the other a teachers' training college at Pannonhalma) and eight grammar schools and the religious houses for Benedictine teachers, 44 elementary schools, and 36 vicarages and chapels.

Of the five demesnes, Tihany was the largest with 6,000 yokes. At the beginnning of this century, the abbey of Tihany had five vicarages and eight elementary schools. (In addition to maintaining the churches and schools and the endowment of the parish priests and teachers, the abbey provided the textbooks for the poor children. When the State School of Balatonfüred was built, the abbey paid half the expenses).

THE DEMESNE OF THE MONASTERY OF TIHANY

The demesne of the abbey of Tihany was situated on the northern and southern shores of Lake Balaton in the Counties of Zala, Veszprém, and Somogy. Five villages (Tihany, Aszófő, Fülöpi, Kis-Szölös, and Örvényes), the public baths of Balantonfüred, a hotel, and a restaurant, which had a good turnover, were on the northern side of the lake. Four farmsteads (Szántód, Tóköz, Jaba, and Kapoly) and two villages (Zamárdi and Endréd) were on the southern side. The abbey sold a small plot near the village of Tósok in 1886 to the village, which had been leasing the land. The small plot of Teleki was sold to the county of Somogy in 1913. The entire demesne was divided into two parts : Tihany with the monastery was the centre in the northern part. The properties of the abbey situated in the county of Somogy had their agricultural centre in Szántódpuszta and their forestry centre in Balatonendréd.

In 1848, the serfs were emancipated. Thus the main problem for agricultural cultivation of the abbey lands in the farmsteads was labour. The number of workers had to be increased. Without enough day labourers and sharecroppers, the abbey tried to obtain workers in other ways. This gave rise to the 'paying off in labour' trend. The abbey gave cleared lands for sharecropping first to its own farmhands. The other sharecroppers had to do some other kind of work for their land, like making hay. This gave importance to motorization, which has also associated with intensive cultivation. In the modernization of production, as formulated by Archabbot Kruesz Krizosztom in 1878, the *conditio sine qua non* was the planting of fodder because stabling of livestock was needed. Less and less pasture land was available because of the separation of the abbey's lands from those belonging to former serfs and because of increasing grain production. To meet the needs of the monks and of the farmhands and other employees, more grain had to be produced to recover the feudal allowance. Grain also had to be marketed. So farmyard manure was very important for enhancing the fertility of the soil and for increasing yields.

For crops, steam engines appeared only in the middle of the 19th century on the lands of the monastery. The motorization of sowing and treshing occurred in the late 1850s and in the 1860s. Chemical fertilizers only began to be used in the beginning of the 20th century.

Only a small portion of the crops could be sold on the domestic market, so merchants came from Austria. During World War I, the main buyers were the government and the Production on War Footing Share Company. The main crops were winter wheat, rye, spring barley, and oats. Root crops (such as potatoes, maize and cattle turnips) and feedstuffs (Burgundy hay, vetch, trefoil, lucern). The growing of sugarbeets lasted only for a short time in the 1910s as it required highly intensive cultivation and needed special knowledge on the part of the workers.

In animal husbandry, sheep farming predominated until the 1870s. The sheep were sold at Pannonhalma in the 1850s and 1860s and then at Tihany. The last period of prosperity in Hungarian sheep farming was in the 1870s, especially for wool. Extensive breeding led to overgrazing; fields were converted to corn production; and foreign, overseas wool led to a rapid decline in sheep breeding. The presence of Rambouillet-type sheep on the abbey's farmsteads shows the decreasing importance of wool production in the 1910s. In cattle breeding, apart from the so-called grey Hungarian cattle (draught animals for ploughing), the red breeds (Montafon, Simenthal) appeared at the turn of the century because of urbanization and the improvement of public transport. The abbey established its own diary operations in 1912 and sold the milk to the creamery at Siófok on the northern shore of Lake Balaton and in the capital. Between the two World Wars, dairying was done at Tihany, especially in the summer. After World War I, steers and fattening pigs (the so-called Hungarian 'mangalica' type, Yorkshire and Berkshire types) were the most important features of animal husbandry in the Somogy district.

The famous halfbreed stud farm of the abbey was at Szántódpuszta. In 1908, one began to breed horses for agricultural as well as transportation purposes. In the 1920s, good carriage horses were bred here, and the abbey sold them from Hungary to as far away as Berlin.

A veterinarian was employed from 1846 on, but the animal keepers often made use of folk medicine.

In the 1860s, to the leasing out of cleared lands was added the leasing out of 'minor royal beneficial interests' (*regale*), such as butcher's stalls, public houses, and mills. The Convent had already suggested in July 1848 that they should hire out the public houses and the inns. In the second half of the 19th century, the abbey had to compensate not only for the loss of the ninth part of crops for the clergy (*nona*) and the tenth part of crops for landowners (*decima*) because of the laws of 1848 but also for the loss of tithes on wine.

They also had to combat the vine pest (*phylloxera*) at the end of the last century. The abbey had its own vineyards in Kóhegy next to Szántódpuszta and in Rózsahegy near Balatonendréd. After 1848, they leased out the public houses and the brandy distilleries (Endréd, Zamárdi, Teleki) and the public house near the ferry as well as the inn at Endréd. The tenants had to sell a certain amount of the abbey's wine. This was possible only until a new law in 1888 declared that issuing liquor licenses was an exclusive right of the State. After the *phylloxera* catastrophe, the vineyards began to be renewed in 1914. Of the wines, such as muscatel, the Hungarian 'kadarka' red wine, the favourites were the table wines, especially the Riesling.

The 'minor royal beneficial interests' were mainly occupied by Jewish tenants, who had excellent relations with the abbey. The abbey bought timber, iron, and metal goods from them as well as oil-seed cake (an industrial fodder). In 1885, these tenants had the right of Balaton fishing.

The abbey became associated with the developing resort industry in Balantonfüred, where it had a hotel, a restaurant, and medicinal baths. Supplying visitors with food at this health resort and around the lake was of minor importance in the abbey's view. Intensive vegetable and fruit production was more characteristic of smallholders. The selling of parcels and plots of land around Balantonfüred and from the former pasture of Zamárdi was important from 1866 on and boomed after 1881. This income created the opportunity of changing the former feudal estate to capitalistic landed property.

The abbey was not averse to maintaining contacts with the

agricultural societies, which existed in every county. In 1871, the abbot permitted a ploughing competition at Szántódpuszta, which was organized by the economic society of Karád (county of Somogy).

THE ECONOMIC MANAGEMENT OF THE DEMESNE

The central economic organization of the Benedictine order in Hungary was critical to the development of the demesne. In 1802, after the temporary suppression after 1786 during the reign of Joseph II, the Order was reinstalled in its previous position. All rights were reserved to the archabbot, including the direction of the economic affairs of the five abbeys (the abbot always resided at Pannonhalma). Each abbey had to contribute to the financial expenses of the Order. In the 19th century, the five abbeys had local economic boards in addition to the Central Economic Committee of the Hungarian Benedictine Order at Pannonhalma. The lands of the Abbey of Tihany in the Somogy district were placed under the central economic direction of the Order in 1905. The farm managers, whose headquarters were at Pannonhalma, also had other official duties, such as the management of the Balantonfüred baths and the central accounting. Local economic supervision remained the task of the steward of the estate of Szántódpuszta.

The farm managers of the Benedictine estates were agricultural and forestry engineers. They had to work in nearly all of the estates belonging to these monasteries and were familiar with all of the stages of agricultural work. In this way, they became acquainted with the entire economic process of the lands of the Order. New farm managers were selected from the demesne's clerics, but there were exceptions if a well-trained, agriculturally skilled manager wanted to work on the estates.

From the 1920s on, some of the monks also attended the Agricultural Academy of Magyaróvár in order to learn how to direct and manage the work of the agricultural employees. The second monk to get a diploma in agricultural studies was Vencel Nagy. After graduating from Magyaróvár, he became the manager of some farmsteads in the Somogy district of the abbey of Tihany and of some farmsteads belonging to the Archabbey of Pannonhalma. He also became the manager of the Order and the head of accounting. His activities with people living in the neighbouring villages of the Order's lands included winter economics courses and the 'silver spike' course of lectures for farmers. As an active member of the Hungarian National Economic Association (OMGE) and of the Chamber of Agriculture, he organized lectures on dairy farming. As a member of the Committee for Distribution of Exports, he supervised the evaluation of fattened animals in Fiume. (At present he has close relations with the Bábolna Agricultural Combinat in the county of Györ-Sopron).

SUMMARY

After the laws of 1848, the monasteries tried to adapt their husbandry to the changed circumstances. After initial difficulties, their demesnes became profitable in the 1880s and the 1890s. This economic development was interrupted during World War I, and there was a large drop in their income in the 1920s. Between the wars, their net receipts exceeded expenses only in the late 1930s, but this was related to the development of the war-time economy.

SOME PROCEDURAL APPROACHES TO COMPARATIVE RESEARCH INTO INTERNAL SOCIO-POLITICAL TENSION
(A Case Study of Separate States in the Twentieth Century)

BORIS GREKOV

INTRODUCTION

Soviet historiography has been engaged in system studies of internal socio-political conflicts only relatively recently. Such studies have become possible thanks to, first, in-depth theoretical research carried out in the Soviet Union into quantification methods applied to historical process studies and, second, special monographs in which these methods were used to treat various aspects of Russia's working-class movement of the late 19th and early 20th centuries as well as some shifts in imperialist Russia's agrarian and industrial development.

A whole complex of system studies in the Soviet Union which deal with internal socio-political tension (SPT) is naturally connected with scientific progress in other countries, in particular with American cliometric research into socio-economic and socio-political progresses. Numerous procedural approaches as well as special studies have been put forward, such as a comparative analysis of revolutions, the elaboration of conflict intensiveness scales, an analysis of the interconnection of internal and external conflicts, and the building of new simulation models statically depicting various internal conflicts in different countries.

The American cliometricians, however, confess that their research into these problems has some gaps. Thus, one of the leading US scholars in this field, Charles Tilly, wrote not long ago that their studies of internal socio-political conflicts in the USA lack dynamic models.

Of late, studies dynamically analyzing internal socio-political tension and internal political stability have appeared in Western Europe. For example, the GLOBUS project treats the dynamics of internal political stability in a systemic unity with a number of international, internal political, and economic factors.

The present work is an attempt to elaborate one of the possible and rather simple ways of modelling socio-political tension (SPT) in dynamics. It is based on the analysis of different economic and political parameters.

Our approach to this problem differs from that of Western cliometricians who are engaged in the analysis of internal conflicts. Unlike American and West European authors who study in detail the structure of a conflict in statics (rarely in dynamics) and the mechanism of interaction of various factors causing a conflict, we prefer to apply a different procedure, the so-called 'indicative scheme' of SPT analysis which includes : a) the system 'conflict', which is the object of research, while the structure of the system for the period of the study is taken as a constant; b) identification within the framework of a given system of subsystem-units fundamental for a system's functioning; c) selection of elements indicators that describe with sufficient fullness the behaviour of subsystem-units; d) the principal system characteristic is a dimensionless integral index assuming that the elements indicators are linearly connected with it; e) subsystem-units are considered to be 'black boxes', i.e. their internal structural ties do not lend themselves to an analysis.

Thus, the author discards the approach that can be tentatively described as a 'simulation of situations' and that would demand the subjective finding of interconnections between all the elements of a political structure or the construction of a comparative 'conflict scale'.

The present work studies SPT dynamically with the help of economic and political indicators for the examples of Russia (1895-1914) and Pakistan (1950-1987). Such a wide spatial and temporal range was not an obstacle to accumulating interesting observations in the comparative analysis of the processes. Both of these countries in the given periods of time underwent a conspicuously dynamic development. Hence, we chose them as convenient 'testing ground' for analyzing various historio-cognitive questions, tasks, retrospective forecasting, as well as some methodological problems.

We can safely say that the results obtained not only present a picture of SPT dynamics that approximates real socio-political processes in these countries but also allow us to treat the procedure as suitable for studying the given complex of problems.

It should be noted that the approach makes it possible to connect internal political crisis with the course of world developments in corresponding regions. Thus, indicative in this respect turned out to be the analysis of the interconnection of internal conflict in Russia in the period from 1895 to 1914 with the progress of Russo-German relations in the same period of time.

We can trace similar phenomena while analyzing the interrelationship between the SPT dynamics in Pakistan and this country's international situation.

The results obtained in comparative studies of internal and external political processes using the above-mentioned procedure lead us to believe that it is expedient to continue work utilizing the 'indicative' method of analysis.

SYSTEMS ANALYSIS OF THE SOCIO-POLITICAL TENSION (STP) IN RUSSIA (1895-1914)

You can hardly find a more dynamic two-decade period in the history of Russia than that between 1895 and 1914, when the revolutionary situation, for the first time in the country's history, had grown into a revolution. It is these years that saw the prerequisites for the victorious February Revolution and then for the triumphant Great October Socialist Revolution.

Therefore, interest in this period of Russia's history is quite legitimate and understandable. We focus our attention on the study of the SPT dynamics and also on the development of separate elements of this system, the political organizations. We also consider some economic parameters that conditioned the growth of the socio-political tension. This range of problems is viewed from the position of a system approach and analyzed with the help of quantification methods. The first element of the SPT model comprises the following indices: 'a total number of those in jail annually' (A) and 'an average daily number of prisoners' (A_2). The second element of the model has the following parameters: the number of troop engagements to aid civilian authorities in the struggle with their own people ('the internal enemy'), the size of investments allocated for supporting and developing the armed forces and the Russo-Japanese war ('the external enemy'). Thus, we have B_1: the number of these troop engagements; B_2: the number of soldiers sent; B_3: the annual expenditures for the army, navy and the Russo-Japanese war.

We examined the periodical press as a third element of the model. To characterize the evolution of this element we used the obvious fact that the number of press organs grew with the upsurge of the revolutionary and liberation movement, while the number of periodical publications closed grew when the reaction reined supreme. Proceeding from this we took as a calculation parameter the ratio of opened press organs to closed ones: C.

Chronologically, the development of elements A, B, C embraces the whole period under investigation. However, the model takes into account some elements of Russia's political structure functions only for some periods considered in the present work. Naturally, they are studied only in the given period of their existence, and in the remaining years they are taken as negligible values.

In March 1906, Russian trade unions were legitimatized for the first time. They started to originate in 1905. Taking into consideration while constructing a model the trade union movement's concentration on the class conflict, we presupposed the existence of a linear relation between the number of trade unions 'D' and the scope of the class conflict.

The October Manifesto of 1905 stipulated a new element in the political structure, the Council of Ministers uniting the activities of all the ministers in tsarist Russia.

Our calculations are based on a value equal to the ratio between the annual number of journals issued by the Council of Ministers intended to suppress the revolutionary movement (E_2) and the total number of journals (E_1). This index (E), in our opinion, most clearly reflects the upsurge of the political struggle in the country.

Setting before ourselves the task of defining a theoretical dimensionless indicator of SPT, we assumed, as 'initial conditions' of the task, that the level of SPT had been growing from 1895 to 1913. Considering the indicator of SPT (let us define it as D) in the systems unity with the above-mentioned elements of the model (A, B, C, D, E), this initial, rough assumption was made more accurate.*

The general dynamics of socio-political tension in Russia in 1895-1913 was investigated to the fullest extent in Soviet historiography. Its essence boils down to the fact that, beginning with the mid-1890s, the revolutionary-liberation movement, permanently on the rise, had reached a rather high level by the 20th century. By this time, a revolutionary situation obtained in the country had grown into the revolution of 1905-1907. The revolution suffered a temporary setback, and the reaction set in later – in 1910 – giving way to a fresh upsurge of a revolutionary activity. The latter's rise had brought about the situation where Russia again found herself on the threshold of a new revolutionary upheaval right before the First World War.

Quantification methods, applied in this article, give us an opportunity to graphically demonstrate this process and supply us with new data about it.

We think that the first 'indicator' of internal political tension can serve as the theoretically calculated dependence of internal political tension on time Z(t), where t is time. Of special importance are the maximums of the given dependence, which are considered to be 'necessary conditions' for the internal political crisis situation. These 'necessary conditions' can be supplemented by a number of 'adequate conditions' that allow us to make a comparative analysis of crisis situations. Such 'adequate conditions' may include : 1) the size of the space below the curve in the maximum area, which testifies to the integral magnitude of a crisis; 2) the absolute dimension of the function at the point of the extremum, which characterizes the sharpness of a crisis; 3) the specific weight of different factor-elements (A, B, C, D, E, etc.) of a political system comprising the given extremum. The next group

* *The procedure:* The redefined system of equations was constructed: $K_1A_1 + K_2A_2 + K_3B_1 + K_4B_2 + K_5B_3 + K_6C + K_7D + K_8E = Z$, where A_1, A_2, B_1, B_2, B_3, C, D, E – elements of the model;
K – coefficients;
Z – indicator of SPT.

This system consists of 19 equations (one equation for each year). First, we substitute in the right part (Z) values taken from 'initial conditions' (linear dependence). Then we find coefficients (K) by the leastsquares method. Having the coefficient (K), one can find the theoretical value Z which differs from the initial conditions. Thus, the initial rough assumption is made more accurate.

of adequate conditions can be defined proceeding from the dynamics of specific weight changes of each factor in various crisis situations. For instance :

$\Delta = A(t_1) - A(t_2)$, where t_1 and t_2 – years of crisis.

The system of indicators of SPT can be used to outline one of the possible ways toward an analysis of alternative developments of the historical process, which has been raised in the latest works by Soviet historians. Specifically, the following 'experiment' was staged : one of the most graphic (from the point of view of the SPT dynamics) factors is a 50 % increase or a 50 % decrease : this factor is the government's repressive actions (the average number of prisoners, troop engagements aiding civilian authorities). The model had only 4 elements, including the two mentioned above, that is, military expenditures and the ratio between the opened and the closed press organs. These were not chance elements, for they characterize the repressive, ideological, and foreign-policy activities of the government. Simulation modelling gave the following result : in the years of revolution the 'decrease' in the repressive actions had no noticeable impact on the SPT. (The situation was no longer under control). In 1909-1910, the calculations speak differently. The 'decrease' in the number of repressive measures brought about a 'splash' of the indicator of SPT (evidence of repression efficiency). The SPT level was analyzed not only on the all-Russia scale, but also on a regional level in different gubernias. Basing ourselves on these data, we examined the level of SPT in 52 European gubernias of Russia (13 economic and socio-political factors for each gubernia in 1901 and 1910) and made a typological analysis of gubernias according to the SPT level (a cluster analysis which gave us an opportunity to draw a map of the SPT level). The estimates testify, in particular, to the growth of SPT in almost all gubernias from 1901 to 1910, which confirms the correctness of the earlier assumption concerning the SPT increase in the given period of time (the initial level). Incidentally, we have attempted to solve a more general task, when as 'initial conditions' the constant was taken.

SYSTEMS ANALYSIS OF SPT IN PAKISTAN (1950-1986)

The procedure used in the analysis of SPT in Russia (1895-1914) served the same purpose in the case of Pakistan in the period of 1950-1986 and once more evidenced its correctness. The data base of political and economic factors was compiled testifying to the dynamics of SPT in the years under review and allowing a short-term forecast. This base consists of two parts : 1) parameters of the political situation received on the basis of expert estimates; 2) indices of the country's economic situation. The sources were official statistical publications.

1. The first set of data consisted of the following elements : a) mass instability : its level was defined by means of expert estimates proceeding from the number killed in political clashes; b) institutional instability : expert estimates were based on a parameter like the forced reshufflings in the upper echelons of power; c) military-political tension : expert estimates were based on the following indices : combat readiness or involvement of specific armed contingents. The result of the procedure we used for the SPT analysis in Pakistan was presented in a graph. On the whole it correctly depicts the well-known political developments at home.

2. The second group of data reflects the potential of the SPT appearance conditioned economically. Empirically (correlation analysis), we selected some economic indicators that indirectly reflected the SPT dynamics. Initially, we took 15 indicators (statistical rows for 1950-1985). Seven were retained : per capita national income, wholesale and retail trade volume, gross national product, the total volume of foreign loans, the US loan, and the USSR loan. Finally, we built a model reflecting the potential stability of SPT in the given country conditioned by economic parameters. Thus estimated, the 'indicator of well-being' serves as an addition to the conclusions obtained with the help of the first data base.

The results obtained were supplemented with the help of the cluster analysis procedures examining coincidence or approximation of characteristics of separate years by parameters collected in the given data base. We obtained the following stable clusters (groups of years) : 1957, 1968, and 1976 : the years preceding the change of regime; 1953, 1970 : the years preceding the critical growth of SPT; 1972, 1978 : the post-crisis restoration of stability; 1958, 1969, 1977 : the changes of regime against the background of crises; 1965, 1971 : the crisis conditioned by foreign-policy complications.

The research into Russia's and Pakistan's political situations is an attempt to construct a dynamic SPT model. However, as was noted above, the results of studies of internal socio-political tension are not always exhaustive if not supplemented by an analysis of the corresponding international situation. The interaction between external and internal conflicts is sometimes very significant.

DYNAMICS OF RUSSO-GERMAN CONFLICT OF 1900-1914

The task was to examine, on the example of the comparative analysis of the Russo-German conflict development in 1900-1914 and SPT dynamics in Russia at the same period of time and to define the connection between them.

The dynamics of the Russo-German conflict were investigated with the help of economic factors. The above-mentioned procedure has brought about indicators of tension in Russo-German ties revealing to some extent the German economic potential in relation to Russia and vice versa. Taking as a basis Lenin's theory of imperialism (Lening knew perfectly well the peculiarities of imperialism before World War I), we included in the model the following elements (all indices were taken for the period 1900-1914): concentration of bank capitals in Germany and Russia; approximate figures for foreign investments in Russian joint-stock banks (British, French and German), figures for Russian and German customs tariffs with relation to each other, and the military expenditures of Germany and Russia.

As a result of using the above parameters (mainly of an economic character), we obtained a theoretical indicator of tension in Russo-German relations for the period 1900-1914. On the whole, the picture thus revealed corresponds to the results of investigation obtained by means of traditional methods. Figures testify that, for instance, in 1904-1906 a considerable increase of the German potential in relation to Russia was outlined, as well as an essential decrease of Russia's potential with relation to Germany, which resulted from the Russo-Japanese war. From 1906 to 1914, there was a trend towards growing Russia's potential in the world arena.

COMPARATIVE ANALYSIS OF INTERNAL AND INTERNATIONAL CONFLICTS

Comparisons of the latter's dependence and the result of analysis of SPT in Russia have been made. Such comparisons were carried out in American historiography on other historical examples and enabled us to confidently state that there is a noticeable correlation between the growing internal socio-political tension in Russia and an increase in potential possibilities of imperial Germany on the international scene.

CONCLUSIONS

The review of the given range of questions leads us to the conclusion that it is expedient to apply, along with other procedures, the above-mentioned technique for investigating general tendencies of internal SPT dynamics of separate countries. This approach also has some prospects for a comparative analysis of dynamics of international and internal political tension. Its positive features are simplicity and demonstrativeness, which facilitate its use and stimulate further, more detailed research.

ETAT ET ENTREPRISES PRIVEES DURANT LA PHASE DE DEVELOPPEMENT DU TRAFIC AERIEN EN ALLEMAGNE, EN FRANCE, EN GRANDE-BRETAGNE ET AUX ETATS-UNIS, 1918-1929

ANDREAS KIESELBACH

Le trafic aérien, branche nouvelle des transports, était initialement associé à la réalisation technique du vol à moteur. Les vols du comte Ferdinand von Zeppelin dans le domaine du matériel 'plus léger que l'air' en 1900 et des frères Wright en 1903 pour le matériel 'plus lourd que l'air' représentèrent une étape décisive.

L'organisation d'un véritable trafic ne démarra qu'à la fin de la première guerre mondiale. Les vols d'essai réalisés dès avant la guerre, tout comme les voyages en dirigeable de la 'Deutsche Luftschifffahrt A.G.' doivent être considérés comme les éléments d'une période expérimentale, caractérisée par le niveau de développement encore très bas des nouveaux moyens de transport. L'amélioration rapide de la technique aérienne qui s'adapta aux besoins de la guerre, et l'extension de centres de production et de recherche se révélèrent indispensables pour mettre sur pied le transport aérien. De plus, tous les pays que nous étudions ici disposaient, à la fin de la guerre, d'un grand nombre de pilotes sans emploi, d'anciens avions militaires et d'une industrie aéronautique qui ne travaillait plus à plein rendement. Tous ces éléments facilitèrent considérablement la création des premiers services aériens réguliers.

Le démarrage de services réguliers incita l'industrie aéronautique à fabriquer de plus en plus d'avions spécialement conçus pour le transport. Les appareils utilisés dans les années précédant la crise économique mondiale de 1929-1933 disposaient le plus souvent d'une capacité moyenne de 4 à 12 passagers; leur vitesse de croisière était de 150 à 180 km/h et leur rayon d'action maximal d'environ 500 à 700 km.

Au cours de cette période, le développement des avions de transport et des installations au sol destinées à la navigation aérienne suivit une ligne assez régulière. Malgré leurs performances encore faibles et leur dépendance à l'égard des conditions météorologiques, de très nombreux types d'avions utilisés avaient, dans l'ensemble, fait leurs preuves sur les services réguliers. Cependant, au début, le problème de la rentabilité ne put être résolu.

Le processus de création du trafic aérien posa de ce fait un problème fondamental. D'une part, le perfectionnement de la technique aéronautique permettait l'ouverture et l'extension de services réguliers. De l'autre, les tarifs aériens restaient élevés et empêchaient le développement d'une demande assez importante pour permettre de couvrir les frais. L'insuffisance des recettes provenant des vols constituait donc, en règle générale, l'obstacle principal à l'exploitation d'un service régulier par une entreprise privée. Une aide substantielle de l'Etat s'avérait par conséquent indispensable pour concrétiser en pratique les possibilités techniques.

C'est ce que découvrirent rapidement, dans les principaux pays industrialisés, les entreprises qui avaient pris l'initiative de lancer des services réguliers. Elles avaient démarré sans aucune aide financière publique car, à la fin de la guerre, les conditions d'un trafic aérien rentable paraissaient assez favorables. Il était alors possible, en effet, d'acquérir du matériel de guerre à un prix très avantageux, ce qui réduisait considérablement le capital minimum nécessaire à la fondation des premières compagnies et à l'ouverture de services réguliers de navigation aérienne. En outre, les indispensables bailleurs de fonds furent rapidement trouvés : le trafic aérien offrait une chance d'investir les profits de guerre dans une branche nouvelle et apparemment appelée à se développer. Cette possibilité intéressait en tout premier lieu l'industrie aéronautique que la fin des hostilités privait de débouchés militaires.

Cependant, les espérances fondées sur la mise sur pied de services réguliers ne se réalisèrent pas immédiatement. Dès les premières années, un soutien financier direct fut octroyé aux entreprises engagées dans les services réguliers.

L'Etat français subventionna le trafic aérien dès le début. Les meilleures conditions pour un développement rapide se trouvaient réalisées aux Etats-Unis d'Amérique : immense potentiel économique, forte demande de transports, immensité du territoire, densité élevée de la population dans les agglomérations. Les compagnies aériennes privées ne pouvaient cependant compter sur une aide financière, car les lois américaines ne permettaient pas les subventions directes. En conséquence, sauf quelques rares exceptions sans incidence majeure sur le marché des transports, les sociétés américaines ne parvinrent pas à mettre en place un service régulier stable. Jusque vers le milieu des années 20, les vols réguliers se limitèrent presqu'exclusivement au service aéropostal entre New-York et San Francisco. Seule une plus forte stimulation de la part de l'Etat, sous la forme d'une allocation relativement élevée pour les envois postaux assurés par les compagnies privées, permit l'essor du trafic aérien dans la seconde partie des années 20. Dès la fin de cette décennie, le trafic aérien occupa aux Etats-Unis une position dominante, en comparaison avec la situation existant sur le plan international.

L'aide financière publique – sous forme de subventions en Europe ou, aux Etats-Unis, de fonds alloués pour le courrier aérien – constituait une sorte d'instrument de régulation permettant de développer des compagnies de navigation aériennes performantes et de mettre en place d'importants services réguliers. Le volume des dépenses publiques affectées à ce domaine eut souvent une influence directe sur l'extension du réseau, sur les prestations aériennes et, par voie de conséquence, aussi sur les résultats obtenus dans le domaine des transports.

En même temps, la stimulation émanant de l'Etat s'étendit aux organisations 'au sol' en rapport avec le trafic aérien : services de télécommunication, émetteurs, centres météorologiques, aéroports, recherche aéronautique. Les résultats enregistrés dans ce secteur ont grandement contribué à l'expansion du trafic aérien. L'intervention de l'Etat se manifesta aussi par des dispositions juridiques multiples visant à réglementer le déroulement des services réguliers. Et ceci s'appliqua tant aux dispositions concernant les subventions et les autorisations qu'à l'adoption de règlements techniques de sécurité, de règles relatives au trafic aérien, de certains droits de contrôle attribués aux autorités etc.

L'internationalisation rapide du trafic aérien ne fut pas la moindre des raisons qui nécessitèrent une action régulatrice publique. Avant la fin de la première guerre mondiale, le principe de la souveraineté nationale sur l'espace aérien avait été admis comme règle juridique de base, obligatoire sur le plan international. Par conséquent, toute mise en place d'une ligne aérienne dépassant les frontières nationales devait être précédée d'accords en la matière. La 'Convention aérienne de Paris' (1919) marqua le début d'une coopération multilatérale. L'Allemagne, exclue en tant qu'ancien adversaire des Etats alliés et temporairement freinée dans l'extension de son trafic aérien par des mesures discriminatoires, recourut à des accords bilatéraux afin de s'organiser sur le plan international. Des règlements spéciaux étaient en vigueur pour le service aéropostal frontalier; après la conclusion de plusieurs conventions internationales, deux accords sur le transport des lettres et des paquets par la voie aérienne furent intégrés dans la 'Convention postale universelle'.

Cet ensemble de mesures régulatrices prises par les divers Etats contribua grandement, dès la veille de la crise économique mondiale, à la mise en place du trafic aérien dans les principaux pays industrialisés tels que l'Allemagne, la France, la Grande-Bretagne et les Etats-Unis d'Amérique.

Les critères suivants caratérisaient nettement le trafic aérien en tant que branche autonome des transports :

1. Le trafic aérien assurait des tâches spécifiques : le transport rapide, sur de longues distances, de passagers, de marchandises et d'envois postaux de grande valeur ou considérés comme urgents. 'Rapide' signifiait, dans ce contexte, plus rapide que les moyens de transports classiques tels que le chemin de fer, le bateau à vapeur ou à moteur et les véhicules automobiles. Pendant la première décennie des services réguliers, l'aire d'utilisation des avions se limitait presque exclusivement au trafic sur distances ultracourtes (jusqu'à 300 km) et, parfois, sur distances courtes (300 à 1.500 km). Les liaisons au long cours qui existaient déjà sous la forme des premières lignes intercontinentales exigeaient toujours des escales, car le niveau de la technnique aéronautique était encore insuffisant.

2. Le trafic aérien utilisait des moyens de transport spécifiques qui s'appuyaient sur un système de voies aériennes interconnectées constituant un réseau autonome. C'est l'avion qui était presque toujours utilisé pour les services réguliers. Les quelques tentatives faites avec d'autres types d'aéronefs furent éphémères. L'organisation au sol (c'est-à-dire l'ensemble des services et des installations de sécurité aérienne, des dispositifs de navigation et des aéroports) atteignit un niveau relativement élevé dès la fin des années 20.

3. Le trafic aérien se caractérisait par des formes d'organisation et par des technologies de transport autonomes. Les compagnies aériennes travaillaient pour leur propre compte; les installations d'aéroports publiques ou privées étaient indépendantes; la réglementation du trafic relevait de diverses autorités publiques et ministérielles ainsi que des premières associations internationales.

Ce qui singularise le trafic aérien, c'est essentiellement le transport par la voie des airs, les formalités inhérentes au fonctionnement des aéroports et la surveillance du trafic aérien.

4. Durant les années 20, le trafic aérien ne présentait pas encore l'aspect d'un trafic de masse. Les résultats obtenus n'étaient pas négligeables, mais restaient en dessous du volume énorme des prestations fournies par les autres branches des transports. On peut cependant considérer que le trafic aérien se trouvait alors définitivement établi, tout au moins en Europe et aux Etats-Unis, puisque des services réguliers de plus en plus complexes fonctionnaient selon un plan bien établi. Les centres européens les plus importants et les grandes villes des Etats-Unis étaient dorénavant réciproquement accessibles par la voie des airs. Le volume de l'offre restait relativement constant ou était en augmentation. Les structures des réseaux se présentaient cependant de manière différente selon les pays, en fonction des intérêts politiques et économiques spécifiques, des objectifs politiques divergents en matière de transport ainsi que des réalités géographiques.

Dans cet ordre d'idées, le trafic aérien allemand se caractérisait par un réseau intérieur assez dense et par l'extension systématique de nombreuses liaisons européennes. Parallèlement, on avait procédé à quelques vols d'essai en vue de se préparer à un trafic aérien vers l'Amérique du Sud et vers l'Asie. Les compagnies françaises exploitaient diverses lignes européennes mais se concentraient surtout sur les itinéraires servant à rejoindre les territoires coloniaux français d'Afrique. Les compagnies britanniques ne disposaient que d'un nombre restreint de lignes destinées au trafic avec le continent européen. La politique de navigation aérienne anglaise était centrée sur la préparation d'un service aérien global, axé sur l'empire britannique. Un premier succès important dans ce domaine fut l'ouverture de la ligne Londres-Karachi. Le trafic américain se limitait principalement à un réseau intérieur performant et très ramifié. Il faut cependant noter que les relations aériennes avec l'Amérique latine avaient déjà débuté par l'ouverture des premières liaisons régulières au départ des Etats-Unis.

Le stade de développement des réseaux et les résultats acquis différaient donc sensiblement dans les divers pays envisagés. En revanche, le processus de centralisation qui s'engagea partout dans le domaine des compagnies de navigation aérienne présenta de nombreux points communs.

Cette centralisation fut précédée par la fondation d'un certain nombre d'entreprises privées de navigation aérienne qui instaurèrent des services réguliers dans chaque pays. Cette phase fut suivie d'un processus très rapide de concentration et de centralisation. Dans un laps de temps de quatre à cinq ans, certaines compagnies se développèrent au point de dominer le marché en pleine extension et d'engager la lutte pour établir un monopole. L'action régulatrice de l'Etat exerça un influence décisive sur l'évolution ultérieure. Le financement des lignes régulières, en particulier, fut d'une importance capitale. Les subventions publiques et les montants élevés alloués pour le service postal constituaient une aide précieuse pour les compagnies aériennes dans leur concurrence avec les branches traditionnelles des transports. Dans les Etats européens envisagés, les subventions aux services réguliers s'élevèrent pendant des années à près de 70 à 80 % des recettes totales réalisées par les compagnies aériennes. Cette politique ne contribua pas peu à une accumulation de capitaux encore favorisée par les concessions et les subventions qui avantageaient les compagnies les plus importantes.

Très rapidement, le processus de centralisation aboutit de ce fait à la fusion des compagnies aériennes, jusqu'alors concurrentes, en une société unique détenant le monopole au niveau national ou par la formation, aux Etats-Unis, de sociétés d'importance comparable. Dans ce contexte, l'intervention plus ou moins intensive ou les pressions des services publics compétents jouèrent une fois de plus un rôle essentiel.

Des compagnies nationales jouissant d'un monopole virent ainsi le jour en 1924 en Grande-Bretagne ('Imperial Airways'), en 1926 en Allemagne ('Deutsche Luft Hansa') et en 1933, à la fin de la crise économique mondiale, en France ('Air France'). Aux Etats-Unis, des compagnies (plus tard appelées les 'Big Four') acquirent en 1930 une position de monopole sur les lignes transcontinentales : vers la même époque, la 'Pan American Airways' obtint un monopole quasi incontesté sur le trafic aérien international américain.

La fondation de ces grandes sociétés fit naître dans les principaux pays industrialisés des relations particulièrement étroites entre l'appareil d'Etat et l'économie privée dans le domaine du trafic aérien. Cela se reflétait dans la répartition des actions entre l'économie privée et l'Etat. Dans les pays européens ainsi qu'aux

Etats-Unis, des commissions ou conseils officiels consultatifs où se regroupaient des représentants de l'Etat, de l'économie privée et des institutions scientifiques, déployèrent une importante activité. Des représentants du gouvernement et des cadres supérieurs des diverses sociétés privées ne manquaient pas de se consulter sur certains problèmes spéciaux.

L'étroitesse de la coopération ou même de l'interdépendance entre l'Etat et l'économie privée varia d'un pays à l'autre dans les principaux Etats industrialisés; elle revêtit aussi divers aspects. Partout cependant cette collaboration fut indispensable pour installer définitivement cette nouvelle branche des transports qu'était le trafic aérien.

CHEMIN DE FER ET RESEAUX D'AFFAIRES EN AFRIQUE OCCIDENTALE : LE DAKAR-NIGER, 1883-1960

MONIQUE LAKROUM

A la fin du XIXe siècle, l'établissement des premières voies ferrées en Afrique de l'Ouest fut non seulement un instrument des colonisation, mais aussi, pour certains industriels français, le moyen d'expérimenter de nouvelles techniques de construction et d'exploitation. Ces programmes influencés par les conceptions saint-simoniennes et encouragés, dès 1879, par le ministère des Travaux Publics connurent leur apogée avec les projets de chemins de fer transsahariens et transafricains.

Cependant ces plans de domination continentale étaient fort éloignés des stratégies élaborées sur place par les militaires. A partir des anciens comptoirs de la côte atlantique, l'itinéraire de ces derniers prenait appui sur les fleuves, voies de pénétration naturelle vers les grands bassins intérieurs du Niger ou du Congo. La première partie de cette étude analyse l'évolution des divers projets de colonisation en Afrique occidentale (chapitre 1) et l'importance croissante des autorités locales dans les choix techniques et économiques qui présidèrent à l'inauguration des voies ferrées (chapitre 2). L'analyse financière des bilans d'entreprise et de la comptabilité publique permet de mieux saisir les divers objectifs et enjeux sous-jacents.

Ces opérations avaient cependant un point commun : leur ignorance des pratiques et des usages du commerce africain hérités de l'ancienne traite coloniale. En opposition aux formes d'organisation et aux méthodes commerciales associées au trafic ferroviaire, ces règles particulières de l'échange, fondées sur la maîtrise du transport, se révèlent peu à peu. L'étude (IIe partie) menée à partir de la correspondance des chambres de commerce et des archives de l'Union coloniale souligne le contraste entre la rigidité des méthodes d'exploitation ferroviaire et la flexibilité des réseaux de traite (chapitre 3).

Outre l'évolution et la répartition des flux de marchandises et de voyageurs, ces sources soulignent l'opposition des systèmes d'organisation et l'impossible association locale des intérêts industriels et coloniaux. L'affrontement, d'abord latent, s'amplifia au lendemain de la première guerre mondiale lorsque le raccordement des divers tronçons ferroviaires constitua un axe de près de 1600 kilomètres, le plus long de l'Afrique occidentale française (chapitre 4). Cette liaison amorçait en effet l'intégration de zones économiques complémentaires et remettait en cause le cloisonnement antérieur des marchés qui était essentiel aux pratiques d'arbitrage des traitants et à la réalisation des profits coloniaux. Les négociants ripostèrent en adoptant et en généralisant le transport automobile et conservèrent ainsi le contrôle des réseaux d'échange intérieurs. Néanmoins, la concurrence rail/route fut vive jusqu'en 1960.

Au-delà des péripéties du conflit, le bilan des programmes ferroviaires ne pouvait être perçu que par une analyse des indices de croissance mesurés sur le long terme entre 1883 et 1957 (IIIe partie). L'évolution du trafic ferroviaire et des ratios techniques et financiers de l'exploitation signalent l'émergence d'une croissance économique interne précoce au cours des premières décennies du XXe siècle, mais indépendante des fluctuations commerciales de la traite arachidière. D'autres facteurs concomitants témoignent de l'amélioration de l'appareil de production et des progrès de productivité dans certains secteurs.

Ce constat permet de nuancer les conclusions fondées sur des indices économiques externes et suggère une lecture critique des méthodes d'analyse reposant sur le calcul des termes de l'échange. Cependant, l'unification des marchés et les écarts régionaux de prix, que la baisse des coûts de transport ferroviaire avait tendance à niveler, n'assurèrent pas pour autant un décollage économique comparable au scénario de la croissance industrielle (chapitre 5).

Au terme de l'étude (chapitre 6), l'explication de cette évolution est replacée dans le cadre des intérêts et des enjeux locaux. L'échec ne semble pas lié en effet à l'inefficacité des techniques ferroviaires et des investissements industriels qui accompagnèrent leur amélioration progressive, mais à leur incapacité à lutter contre des formes de croissance parallèles et concurrentes aux finalités et aux principes divergents. Ainsi l'accroissement quantitatif des échanges n'entraîna pas de changements profonds des systèmes économiques et sociaux africains.

Car l'histoire des chemins de fer africains oscilla sans cesse entre le réel et le possible. Le second nous est singulièrement plus familier que le premier : il y eut tant de projets, tant de plans et de programmes établis à partir du rail qu'ils finissent par cacher, sous l'abondance des documents élaborés, la résistance discrète mais têtue des réalités. Ce sont elles pourtant qui finalement l'emportèrent. Par contrecoup, l'utilité et l'efficacité des innovations apportées furent mises en cause. La rapidité du transport, la régularité du trafic, l'augmentation des quantités déplacées, tout cela parut bien limité par la rigidité des tarifs, la fixité de l'itinéraire et les contraintes des chargements.

Les techniques sont ce que les hommes en font et le rail en Afrique fut d'abord l'expression d'une volonté étrangère plus que la réponse à des besoins internes. Mais est-ce suffisant pour conclure à l'inadéquation essentielle de ce mode de transport aux économies locales? Aujourd'hui le procès est souvent bien rapidement instruit : tout ce qui est 'exogène' est inadapté et l'on oublie les lents processus d'ajustement nécessaires aux systèmes techniques et économiques pour assimiler la nouveauté.

L'analyse de ces phénomènes requiert la longue durée et ce n'est qu'au terme d'une évolution quasi séculaire que la sanction de l'échec paraît s'imposer. Encore faut-il expliquer ce terme car avant d'être l'aboutissement, il fut d'abord l'enjeu. La mise en exploitation des voies ferrées, par les réactions et les oppositions de plus en plus vives qu'elles suscitèrent, révèlent les pratiques et les valeurs des négociants et traitants locaux, les jeux de l'échange et les règles du profit marchand.

En Afrique occidentale, depuis trois siècles, les maisons de commerce bordelaises drainaient les produits de l'intérieur grâce à un réseau complexe de relations tissées avec les transporteurs africains. Des rives sahariennes à l'orée de la zone forestière, les caravanes acheminaient les marchandises et les hommes. Les comptoirs de la côte avaient survécu en se reliant aux circuits de ce grand commerce continental et la lente reconversion de la traite au cours du XIXe siècle ne put s'opérer que grâce aux circuits préétablis, à cette association ancienne entre des activités complémentaires mais différentes.

La collaboration reposait sur un principe commun : les règles de l'échange étaient régies par celles du transport. La valeur s'établissait en chemin et non sur des marchés permanents; le conditionnement et la mise en charge toujours complexes et sujets à marchandage établissaient les prix. Le commerce était un trafic. Les profits tenaient à cette mise en contact sélective et temporaire de zones de production. Car la discontinuité était le mode d'organisation essentiel de ces réseaux de transport et d'échange : elle seule permettait de contrôler la rareté, fondement de toute valeur.

L'irruption d'un nouveau mode de transport comme le chemin de fer remit en cause des mécanismes délicats. Ce n'est pas tant l'innovation qui en elle-même en compromit le fonctionnement – l'automobile quelques décennies plus tard fut immédiatement adoptée et intégrée aux pratiques anciennes – que le système de circulation et la réorganisation des flux qu'elle supposait. La menace n'apparut cependant pas tout de suite, car le rail fut longtemps l'arme des militaires, moyen logistique essentiel qui permit avec peu d'homme et peu de moyens de porter la guerre jusqu'à la boucle du Niger.

Ainsi les réalisations économiques que l'on attendait de l'établissement des voies ferrées furent limitées. Tant que les deux tronçons ferroviaires du Dakar-Saint Louis et du Kayes-Niger restèrent séparés, les modifications de trafic conservèrent un caractère régional qui ne compromettait pas le fonctionnement des circuits du commerce de traite. Mais dans le même temps, les industriels métropolitains se désengagèrent peu à peu de l'exploitation des voies ferrées africaines, entreprises difficiles à rentabiliser et où la capacité de gestion était de plus en plus circonscrite par les interventions administratives. Les grands projets de transsaharien demeuraient mais l'espoir d'emporter de nouveaux chantiers était limité par la généralisation des constructions en régie.

Dès 1905, l'affirmation d'un pouvoir local autonome, le gouvernement général de l'A.O.F., modifia les enjeux. Plus au contact des négociants, mais aussi plus sujet à leurs pressions directes, il développa un projet de colonisation agricole le long des axes ferroviaires existants et étendit ce front pionnier grâce à la reprise de la construction du troncon central entre Thiès et le Niger. Certes l'extension de la culture de l'arachide réactiva les échanges d'un système de traite en déclin, mais la liaison ferroviaire directe entre Dakar et le Niger, achevée en 1923, remit également en cause le compartimentage des marchés et la maîtrise des flux et des débits essentiels aux pratiques d'arbitrage spatiaux et temporels qui assuraient le profit colonial.

Aussitôt le conflit éclata. Dès 1925, la vivacité et la promptitude des réactions sont révélatrices. Sans doute les conditions techniques de la jonction n'étaient-elles pas idéales. Bien des installations se révélèrent insuffisantes et l'ensemble de la ligne dut être reconstruite par étape. Cependant, loin de s'apaiser avec la mise en œuvre progressive de solutions techniques de plus en plus efficaces, l'hostilité des milieux d'affaires s'amplifia. Leurs interventions par l'intermédiaire de l'Union coloniale furent dès les années trente coordonnées et dirigées, au niveau local, par la Chambre de commerce de Dakar. Au-delà des motifs multiples mais récurrents de conflit (les tarifs, les avaries dues au transport, les rythmes d'évacuation de l'arachide) transparaît une opposition plus profonde mettant en cause non seulement le profit et le pouvoir, mais aussi l'existence même du monde de la traite.

Comprendre ces logiques opposées requiert une observation particulière. Par contraste avec les formes d'exploitation ferroviaire et l'organisation économique qui lui est associée, il fallait décoder les règles du transport, les fondements de la valeur, les principes de l'échange propres au milieu colonial. Et tout d'abord saisir les mouvements, comprendre les relations et les interactions entre chacun des protagonistes.

Aux tissus diffus et denses des connexions multiples et mouvantes suscitées par la traite, le rail imposait une canalisation unique et linéaire des flux. Aux transports d'éclatement et à la flexibilité des circuits de bouclage nécessaires au commerce, il opposait un trafic de transit exigeant un drainage préalable et la concentration des activités.

A la profusion et à la multiplication des formes de circulation et d'échange, il infligeait une sélection fondée sur la hiérarchie des centres urbains et des itinéraires. Il contrariait le savant compartimentage et la segmentation des marchés indispensables à la réalisation des profits par la fusion et l'intégration progressive de zones de production complémentaires. Enfin, dans cet espace économique lache et mouvant, il incarnait, par ses effets comme par son mode d'exploitation, l'emprise d'un pouvoir centralisateur.

Ainsi ce ne fut pas le heurt de la tradition et de la modernité, de l'archaïsme et du progrès technique, mais au contraire la compétition entre deux formes de croissance : l'une sélective et cumulative sur le modèle de développement industriel européen, l'autre procédant par multiplications et reproductions successives des mêmes formes d'activités. Dès lors, les gains de productivité offerts par les améliorations des modes de transports permirent l'accroissement du nombre des intermédiaires; la réduction des coûts et des prix que l'on pouvait espérer ne se réalisa pas; bien plus, l'exploitation ferroviaire elle-même fut de l'intérieur absorbée par ce processus qui compromit toute amélioration de la productivité du travail.

La suprématie du commerce, les principes de l'échange demeuraient et les diverses modalités de la croissance se diffusèrent sans entraîner de changements profonds des systèmes économiques et sociaux : l'évolution n'était ni tout à fait la même, ni tout à fait une autre. L'extension des voies ferrées n'avait pu susciter les formes et les valeurs d'un développement industriel. Mais peut-on créer sans détruire?

URBANIZATION AND INDUSTRIALIZATION IN BOHEMIA BEFORE 1914

JAROSLAV LÁNIK

Analysis of the urbanization process in Europe in the 19th and 20th centuries yields a sufficient volume of evidence indicating that urbanization was uneven in individual countries and areas. There have been significant differences in the periods of urbanization and its forms, conditions, and degrees. The aim of the present study is to clarify some aspects of town development in Bohemia and the entire settlement system, which is called 'indirect urbanization'. The study concentrates on the period between 1830 and 1914, with the emphasis on the time between the end of the 1860s and the outbreak of World War I.

A narrow definition of urbanization is used for the purposes of the study. Urbanization is regarded as one of the forms of change in the spatial organization of society in which there is a concentration of population in large towns and in which the proportion of urban population increases over that of the rural population. Thus the dynamics of the changes in the settlement system are examined from both the spatial and the temporal points of view, and the individual components of town growth are analyzed. Special attention is given to the relationship between industrialization and urbanization, with the branch structure of industry, the concentration tendencies, and industrial development as a whole being investigated.

The number of town inhabitants began to grow in the 1830s and the 1840s, with more pronounced growth occurring in the 1860s. Town growth was due primarily to immigration. The population-replacement ability of towns up to the beginning of the 1890s was quite low due to high mortality rates, particularly neonatal and infant mortality. In some industrial centres, half of the children died before reaching the age of five years. Only in the first half of the 1890s was there a significant decrease of mortality: before 1910, child mortality decreased by about a half. From the middle of the 1890s to about 1905, all of the towns had absolute and relative natural population increases. This period, however was short. As early as the second half of the 1890s, there was a drop in the birth rate. Towns with particularly low gross birth rates suffered from population drops in some pre-war years due to natural decrease.

The emerging large industrial areas in the Northern Bohemian softcoal basin and the areas with the textile industry absorbed vast amounts of labour. Gradually, more and more centres were created in these areas. The migration streams were directed to specific centres, which meant limitations on town development because of the small number of immigrants. The migration base of the largest Czech towns only rarely exceeded a radius of 50 km, and the bases of neighbouring towns tended to overlap considerably.

One of the factors that influenced the growth of the largest Czech towns was the very small area of the *cadastre.* Therefore, growth shifted to the surrounding communities. After the 1870s and particularly the 1880s, some towns formed conurbations, but even these were rather small, and often the influence of the towns (taken in terms of the population increment of the surrounding communities) was restricted to the communities within 3 km of the conurbation centre and very exceptionally any further. One utilization aspect is the method of housing. The large Czech towns (with the exception of Prague and some towns of the Prague conurbation and, to a degree, Plzeň) did not build blocks of flats, i.e., buildings with more than 20 flats. The number of buildings with more than 10 flats is low. The size of the buildings is also reflected in the number of storeys : there were few with two, three, or more storeys. Analysis of the housing showed that cellars and attics were used in the industrial centres of North Bohemia, West Bohemia, and Liberec and that most of the flats used by the poorer strata were overcrowded. The boom phase manifested itself mostly in the renting of these flats to tenants and lodgers and not in new housing construction. Urban-type housing was present in Prague and some of the towns belonging to the Prague conurbation.

The process of urbanization in Bohema was influenced considerably by the 'branch' structure of Czech industry.

The significance of the individual branches for urbanization in Bohemia can be determined on the basis of the 1910 census, the results of which are published for all towns with more than 20,000 inhabitants. These towns were the important centres of commerce and industry and also the centres of administration and culture.

Their function is manifested in the different occupational structures of the inhabitants as compared with those of smaller towns and communities. Significant differences in representation of the individual branches in communities below 20,000 inhabitants and in those with more than 20,000 inhabitants can be found in five different branches. The mining industry represented a considerable share of the communities with less than 20,000 inhabitants (6 %). It had little significance for the growth of towns with more than 20,000 inhabitants (only 1.7 %), while the stone and oil industry (9.9 %, 4.0 %) and the textile industry did affect town growth. The share of the building industry in the smaller communities was high, but this was due to the term of the census (31 December), i.e., the period in which the seasonal immigrants were back in their permanent residential areas. Metal working and mechanical engineering participated significantly to the growth of towns with more than 20,000 inhabitants (13.2 % as compared with 7.3 % for the communities with less than 20,000 inhabitants). But in such towns, too, the greatest number of the inhabitants worked in the textile and clothing industries. Significant positions were continuously held by the food industry.

More significant representation can be seen in the differences between the individual branches when the share of the working population is examined not as a whole but separately for each branch. The chemical industry was concentrated in towns with more than 20,000 inhabitants and those in the Prague conurbation. In the census period, they accounted for one third of the working population in the chemical industry of Bohemia. Mechanical engineering was also centered in the large towns (28 % of the working population) as was the clothing industry (25.8 %). Textiles, mining, and metallurgy, however, were scattered, as was the stone and soil industry in particular; only 5 % of the working population of this branch lived in the large towns.

The analysis of the branch structure of industry in the individual towns made it possible to determine its effect on urban growth. Some of the largest towns also had mostly a single-branched structure. This holds true for Aš and Varnsdorf, of which 70 % and 60 %, respectively, of the population worked in the textile industry. The favourable multiple-branch structure of industry was found in large regional centres : České Budějovice, Plzeň, Ústí nad Labem, Kolín, and Pardubice. Analysis of the occupations of the inhabitants of the largest towns in Bohemia can produce a typology :

I. Mono-functional industrial towns

a) The proportion of the population working in industry reached more than 70 % of the economically active inhabitants. At the same time, the industrial structure was dominated by one branch : Aš, Varnsdorf
b) The proportion of the population working in industry reached more than 60 % of the economically active inhabitants. In these towns, too, only one branch dominated but less than in the first case : Kladno, Jablonec nad Nisou.

II. Polyfunctional towns

a) With considerable industrial representation, the proportion of the population working in industry reached 50 % to 60 % of the economically active population. This subdivision may be further divided as follows :
   1. Towns with a significant representation in transportation, trade, and services : Most, Ústí nad Labem, Chomutov
   2. Towns with a significant representation of administration and cultural functions : Kutná Hora
   3. Town with a significant representation of agriculture
b) Industrial towns with a significant representation of other functions. The share of the population working in industry reached less than 50 % of the economically active. Generally, they are large regional centres : Plzeň, České Budějovice, Liberec, Chab, Pardubice, Kolín, Žatec
c) Towns with the least developed industry, generally with a significant absence of heavy industry, but with some special functions : Teplice-Šanov, Karlovy Vary.

The problem of the relationship between urbanization and industrialization is closely connected with the periodicity of the urbanization process.

1. The beginning of the 1830s. This period is marked by the beginning of changes in the settlement structure. Because of the

low number of towns with more than 10,000 inhabitants and the strong position of old regional centres, this period is taken to be the preparatory one for urbanization.

2. The beginning of the 1870s to the 1880s and 1890s is taken to be the initial phase of urbanization. In this period, the basic disintegration of the settlement system into two parts is observed. The beginning of the town conurbations occurs, and the number of towns with more than 10,000 inhabitants grows. The traditional centres are repressed.
3. The turn of the 1880s and the 1890s to 1914 represents the phase of urbanization development. The North-South polarity was established and extended; town conurbations developed; the group of the largest Czech towns was completed and considerably stabilized. The conspicuous slow down of town growth in those with more than 10,000 inhabitants in the first decade of the 20th century reflects the insurmountability of many limitations on Czech town growth. Moreover, the insufficient representation of the 'town branches' in the branch structure of the Czech economy prevailed, and branches that led to territorial and not urban concentration dominated (the textile and mining industries). The strong positions were held by branches that used seasonal labour and thus helped to preserve the old settlement structure (construction and the sugar industries). No significant changes in the concentration of industrial production occurred. In the first decade, the rotation of booms and crises was observed. In Bohemia, the small and medium-sized towns grew and so retarded the urbanization process.

FOREIGN CAPITAL AND THE ST. PETERSBURG INTERNATIONAL COMMERCIAL BANK IN THE 1880s AND EARLY 1890s

SERGEI LEBEDEV

This subject was chosen as a thesis topic for two reasons. First, private commercial banks played an important part in the industrialization of Russia. Second, the Russian banks and especially the St. Petersburg International Commercial Bank (ICB) promoted the inflow of foreign capital into the country.

In the thesis, an attempt has been made to establish the role of the ICB in international banking groups operating within the sphere of Russia's state credit (which absorbed a great part of the foreign capital before the industrial upsurge of the second half of the 1890s). This is why the attention is focused on relations within issue consortia expressed by the system of participations in Russian loan deals, that is to say, on the entire complex of interrelations of the government, railway companies, and Russian and foreign banks. The history of the ICB and its foreign ties is considered with due regard for the main events of Russian foreign policy – deterioration of relations with Germany and rapprochement with France.

The thesis (188 pages) consists of an introduction, four chapters, a conclusion and appendices comprising a bibliography, a list of sources and tables.

The main body of the work begins with the description of the origin of the ICB, its organizational techniques and its history from when the bank started its operations in 1869.

The method used for the study of the ICB's foreign business relations in 1880 is the analysis of the Bank's business correspondence and consortia documents. This is because, of all the accounting documents of that time, only the annual balance sheets, which were usually published before general meetings of the shareholders, have survived. In these balance sheets, the correspondent accounts, which are of great value for establishing the share of foreign capital in *circulating assets,* are represented in general outline. Thus, one can only trace a tendency, and nothing can be said about nationality or the firms that had deposits in the ICB. For example, from the end of November 1895 until the end of the year with a possible prolongation, the ICB accepted 5 million marks at 4.25 % interest from Mendelssohn & Co. And vice versa, in case of low prices for money in St. Petersburg, the ICB could keep its cash in Berlin. (In the second half of June 1879, ICB ceded 18 million marks in cash at 3.5 % interst to the Dresdner Bank) (Lemke, 1984, pp. 172 ff.).

The assessment of foreign participation in the *fixed capital* of Russian banks is often based on lists of shareholders who presented shares at the annual general meetings. Such methods of assessment are usually used in view of the difficulty of counting the distribution of shares inside and outside the country. Since only less than a half of all shares were presented at general meetings in the 1880s, lists of shareholders cannot be used to determine the foreign share of the ICB's fixed capital at that time. Moreover, one should bear in mind that, on the eve of a meeting, the Bank would have at its disposal its Russian and foreign business friends' shares and votes granted as favours.

Thus, by presentation of shares one can only judge foreign influence on the decisions of general meetings relatively and there is always some exaggeration. In the 1870s (up to 1879), the greatest amount of shares was hold by the *Österreichische Kreditanstalt,* the chief intermediary in the distribution of ICB's shares issued in 1872. In the 1880s major foreign shareholders did not present their shares for participation at the meetings. After the 1870s, the greatest amount of shares was in the possession of one of the richest Russian families, the Stroganov family, whose business manager N.N. Antsiferov was the Chairman of ICB's board of directors since 1876.

Russian banks that used Western capital, management experience, and operational techniques willingly invited foreigners, primarily Germans by birth (Germany was Russia's chief trading partner). It was the practice to invite people with thorough European banking experience to occupy important posts in bookkeeping and correspondence and people who ran their own entreprises or had ties with solid local firms to occupy posts of trustees and directors (when ICB's branches were involved). Portraits of bank directors of the period under review, L. Laski and A. Rothstein, are given in the thesis. The peculiarity of the ICB as the *banque d'affaires* was its close ties to a circle of major Russian and foreign bankers and rentiers. The chapter and appendices give some detailed information about them.

According to the statement of the Bank's founders and plans of the Ministry of Finance, the main task of the ICB was to provide credit for Russian exports. In the 1880s, the exporting cities of Odessa and Riga and the main importing city, Moscow, had been applying to the St. Petersburg stock exchange for selling and buying bills of exchange. The Ministry of Finance and railway companies also satisfied their needs in this respect there. By this time, ICB's profits from exchange transactions totalled over a million roubles a year. However, even among St. Petersburg banks, the ICB was noted for its special interest in stock exchange operations. At the start of its activities, the ICB was the first among St. Petersburg business banks to begin developing on-call operations together with fixed date loans, thus providing credit for the stock-jobbing of its clients. Since 1878, on-call operations became the biggest, after correspondents, item of the assets. Until the mid-1870s, ICB's operations were rather successful. By 1875, the annual turnover reached 2.9 bln. roubles. Following the example of the Volga-Kama Bank, the ICB opened its two Southern branches, which provided credit for the sugar trade. The sugar boom ended in 1878. It was followed by a crisis and 737,000 roubles of dubious debts were written off the balance. In the 1880s, the Bank's regular operations became more stable: discounts totalled not more than 9 mln. roubles a year, loans for securities amounted to 11-17 mln. roubles of which on-call loans made up 9-16 mln. roubles. During the same period at the expense of liability correspondents, circulating capital increased from 9-11 mln. roubles in the early 1880s to sums exceeding 30 mln. roubles by the early 1890s.

In general, after the 1880s, a rapid growth of correspondent accounts in the balance is observed. This was undoubtedly connected with the expanded relations with foreign partners and issue operations, which greatly affected the annual profit.

The thesis then examines the question of ICB's participation in issue consortia of private railway bonds in the 1880s and early 1890s. The ICB and German banks were drawn together, not only by their participation in its capital but also by the similarity of their business policy, a special interest in railway issues. At least since 1872, being a major shareholder of several societies, ICB had been making use of railway companies' deposits (loan receipts). The director of the ICB, L. Laski, also occupied the post of director of the Rostov-Vladikavkaz railway. The Bank held strong positions in the Southwest Railway Co from the day of its foundation in 1878. Moreover, V.A. Polovtsev, Chairman of the main society of Russian railways, headed the boards of the ICB and the Russian Bank for Foreign Trade. Thus, the ICB had an opportunity to influence the activities of major Russian railway companies, and foreign banks that participated in issuing Russian railway bonds had to reckon with this.

The ICB was a member of the group of the *Disconto-Gesellschaft* which headed the railway issues in the mid-1880s.

By the late 1880s a group of Russian banks was formed for such operations. The agreement of 1881 between the ICB and the Russian Bank for Foreign Trade marked the beginning of the formation of this group. In 1882, Russian banks joined the consortium of the Ivangorod-Dombrovsk Railway bonds in order to exercise its member's right. In October 1884, a protocol was signed. In the forthcoming issues of bonds by three railway companies and in the sphere of Russian finances in general, the protocol fixed a 40 % participation for the Russian group (the ICB and the Russian Bank for Foreign Trade) and a 60 % participation for the German group (the *Disconto-Gesellschaft* and M.A. Rothschild & Söhne), and provided that a separate agreement was to be signed for every deal. The German partners of the ICB also granted participations in foreign railway loans.

In 1885, owing to international tensions, the rate of exchange of Russian securities dropped, and friction arose between the *Disconto-Gesellschaft* and the ICB, the latter saying that Mendelssohn & Co complied with its regulations more favourably. For example, for subparticipation in the same loan of 1887, the ICB was charged by Mendelssohn & Co and the *Disconto-Gesellschaft* 1/4 % and 1 % respectively. The *Disconto-Gesellschaft*, which headed the consortium, could impose stricter conditions for the ICB than Mendelssohn & Co, which sought the support of the ICB to improve its positions in Russia. In February 1889 a consortium for state and consolidated loans was formed. The ICB, the St. Petersburg Discount Bank, Bleichröder, the *Disconto-Gesellschaft,* and M.A. Rothschild participated in it. In 1892, a Russian syndicate consisting of the ICB, the Russian Bank for

Foreign Trade, the Discount Bank (the agreement had been reached in 1890), the Volga-Kama bank, and the Merchant Bank commenced its issue operations. The formation of the issue syndicate of Russian banks was caused by the closure of foreign money markets after the failure of the 3 % loan of 1891. At the same time, it reflected the growing capacity of the home market on the eve of the industrial upsurge in the mid-1890s.

ICB's position in the consortium was not always that of executing the orders of a foreign leader. It often headed Russian participants in gold loans. In deals arranged in credit roubles, it could not, using its foreign connections, push aside other Russian banks with close ties to railway companies.

The ICB played an important role in the conversions of state and mortgage bonds. This part of the thesis deals with the history of projects and the course of conversions of Russian metallic (gold) loans in the period from 1884 to 1891. The difference of opinion and policy on that matter of Finance Ministers N.Ch. Bunge and I.A. Vyshnegradsky is mentioned here. The struggle around conversions between the two groups, the consortium of the Rothschilds and the syndicate of the *Banque de Paris et des Pays-Bas (Paribas)* is also dealth with.

The 1887 agreement on the conversion of the securities of the Mutual Land Credit Company marked the beginning of regular relations between the ICB and Bleichröder, which previously had belonged to different groups. The syndicate united yesterday's rivals : Bleichröder attempted to restrict the *Disconto-Gesellschaft*'s participation in the operation, and the Discount Bank carried out its operations sometimes ignoring the fact that it caused damage to its partners. Nevertheless, in the autumn of 1887, A.I. Zak, the director of the Discount Bank, declared that his bank and the ICB would conduct talks on all important issues jointly. The union of these banks remained in force irrespective of their relations with Bleichröder and manifested itself in their joint participation in loans in the late 1880s and early 1890s. However, further relations between the two banks remained rather complicated.

In November 1887, the German money market was closed to Russian loans, and the subscription to conversion loans was allowed only in exchange for old securities. The ban (lifted in October 1894) was imposed only on Russian valuables and was an act of hostility towards Russia, which commenced the rapprochment with France. Conversions in 1888-91 were carried out by the two groups that had sought them as early as 1886-87: the Rothschilds and Paribas-Hoskier. The ICB was a member of both groups. Between 1884 and 1889, it mediated in finance ministers' talks on opening the French money market. During the period of conversions the role of Russian banks in syndicates grew considerably due to the strengthening of the home market which was taking up in its 'firm hand' a part of the metallic loans after their expulsion from Germany. Being the leader of the Russian group of the consortium, the ICB drew the ramified state bank machinery into the placing of metallic loans in provinces and enjoyed government protection. The ICB could be included in the consortium 'at the finance minister's will'. At the same time, the ICB conducted negotiations with the Ministry of Finance on behalf of the consortium.

The history of the issue of the Russian 3 % gold loan of 1891 is shown in connection with the Rothschilds and *Paribas* syndicates' policy towards Russia in 1891, the year when the Russo-French consultative alliance pact was signed. The external loan of 1891 completed I.A. Vyshnegradsky's series of conversions and was the first such experience for S. Witte, who became Finance Minister in 1892. The director of the ICB, A. Rothstein, played a special role as an organizer and mediator in this operation. The Bank, which took part in an international speculation in Russian securities, played a double game in it, being a member of a bond issue syndicate and, at the same time, using government information. When the first branch of the Russian Bank for Foreign Trade opened in Paris in 1889, Russian banks and banking houses used it for massive speculation. The ties between the home money market and foreign stock exchanges are also considered in this part of the thesis. The experience gained during conversions of internal loans showed that the finance minister had rather limited freedom of manoeuver on the home market, but at the same time, he possessed a formidable weapon for exercising pressure upon foreign bankers – Russian gold deposits.

After the failure of the 1891 loan the French money market was closed for new Russian loans for some time. And since the issue of bonds in England and Germany was impossible, it had to rely on the domestic market only. Syndicates for the issue of loans in credit roubles were headed by Russian banks, but foreign friends were granted subparticipation. At the same time foreign banks were giving the ICB subparticipation in their deals outside Russia. In connection with this, the German historian H. Lemke notes that the ICB was content with a minor subparticipation (0.5 %) which major German banks usually rejected (Lemke, 1984, p. 162). However they never rejected similar subparticipation in Russian deals that the ICB granted them. Subparticipations considerably changed the correlation of quotas for syndicate members. It turned out that real distribution of Russian metallic securities in the country could have been much higher than the quota for Russian syndicate members.

The thesis concludes that the ICB's dependence on foreign banks was not constant even in the 1880s. Although banking underwent considerable internationalization, the competition among major banks was not along the lines of their nationalities. Actually, it was the struggle of international banking groups. Before 1887, the ICB participated in operations of the *Disconto-Gesellschaft* group and, after establishing regular relations with Bleichröder and the Rothschilds, it took firm positions in this international group (*Disconto* was also in it). The ICB continued to maintain relations with its German partners and the Rothschilds and, at the same time, it participated in a competing syndicate, Paribas-Hoskier (admittedly the Bank's position in this group was more modest). This gave it an opportunity to pursue an independent policy. Thus, the freedom of initiative of Russian banks that resulted from the prevailing 'participation system' existed as early as the close of the 1880s and not only in the ensuing period as has been represented in literature. Relations among banks are much more complicated than one-dimensional 'dependence-independence'. Tangles of interests and participation in each other's deals are characteristic of their relations. The development of the participation system at the close of the nineteenth and the outset of the twentieth century resulted in new relations between banks and industry (direct interest of the parties concerned in each other's business).

And so, in the ICB, we find a Russian version of the *banque d'affaires,* the speculative bank that by the twentieth century had developed into a universal type.

REFERENCES

H. Lemke, 'Verbindungen der Petersburger Internationalen Handelsbank zu deutschen Banken Ende des 19. Jh.', *Jahrbuch für Geschichte der sozialistischen Länder Europas*, 28 (Berlin, 1984).

The St. Petersburg International Commercial Bank's report on operations in 1882 (St. Petersburg, 1883).

THE DEVELOPMENT OF ELECTRICITY SUPPLY IN FINLAND A CASE STUDY OF TECHNOLOGY TRANSFER

TIMO MYLLYNTAUS

The hypothesis of my thesis is derived from the general literature on technology transfer. According to it, a less developed country can rapidly achieve marked results in technology transfer only by relying extensively on the direct involvement of foreign suppliers of technology. Putting faith mainly in domestic entrepreneurship in technology transfer is doomed to fail, because this approach is considered a slow, inefficient and roundabound method for a latecomer to promote industrialization.

In studying the transfer of electrical technology to Finland, we can distinguish eight different channels through which foreign know-how was adopted in the country. The transfer channels concerned were direct foreign investments, the importation of machinery and equipment, the purchase of turn-key plants from foreign companies, the purchase of foreign licences and patents, joint-ventures with foreign companies, the recruitment of foreign specialists, the studies of nationals in foreign technical institutions and other educational visits abroad and finally the utilization of the low cost diffusion of easily accessible technology.

In the late nineteenth century, Finland was a part of the rural periphery of the European continent. It was an agrarian, sparsely populated country which belonged to the bottom third of European countries in terms of GDP per capita. It had no research laboratories for further development of foreign innovations. The country had no strong, modern manufacturing industries nor did it possess an army of capable, well-educated engineers. Nevertheless, rather early on it became one of the most electricity-intensive countries.

The central question in my thesis is why Finland succeeded in electrifying its economy quicker than one might expect on the basis of its economic development.

The importation of the first dynamo in 1877 opened up the age of heavy electrical engineering in Finland. In the subsequent decades, electricity supply was increased by the activities of manufacturing firms, private and municipal electricity supply companies. The role of the government was inconspicuous in promoting electrification up to the early 1920s, when the construction of the state-owned Imatra hydroelectric power plant was started. The government became more closely involved in electricity supply between 1939 and 1949 when the economy and energy supply were strictly regulated. In the postwar decades, the government financed power plants built by its own companies as well as the projects carried out by private companies. It granted loans and subsidies for rural electrification as well. In any case, the government's involvement was not so embracing as in many other Western European countries; for example, the electricity supply system was not nationalized. The ownership structure of the Finnish electricity supply industry is a mixture between private, municipal and government-owned companies.

The manufacturing industry dominated the consumption of electricity in Finland. It needed electricity first of all for mechanical power, i.e. – for driving electric motors. Electro-metallurgical and electrochemical industries developed slowly. The electrification of railways started very late – in the late 1960s. The distribution of electricity from supply utilities to households began in 1884. By 1938 just under 60 % of all households were wired for electricity and by 1977 the figure had risen to 99.5 %. For a long time, households, however, used electricity merely for lighting and their share of the total consumption remained very modest. Various electrical household appliances became available in the interwar years, but it was not until from the 1950s that they were in general use in the country. The diffusion of electrical household appliances and electric space heating was brisk in the 1960s and 1970s. Consequently, the structure of electricity consumption became diversified in a rather short period.

As early as in 1900, Finland generated and consumed approximately the same amount of electricity per capita as Britain, France or Italy, for instance. During the first two decades of the century, Finland was left behind these countries, but in the interwar years it leapt amidst the foremost electricity using countries (in per capita terms). In World War II, Finland probably lost more of its generating capacity than any other country in Europe. Nevertheless, by the early 1970s it restored its prewar place in the rank of electricity consuming countries in the world. There are very few countries which have managed to increase its electricity output quicker than Finland from the late 1910s to the 1970s. Between 1890 and 1977, the annual growth of total electricity consumption was on average 12.7 %, whilst the growth rate was 8.6 % in the period 1920-1977.

The relative rapid electrification of Finland was not based on indigenous technical innovations. None of the great inventors related to electrical technology were from Finland, although surprisingly many of them were brought up in Scandinavia, Eastern and Southern Europe. The peripheral location of those countries could not inhibit inventive activity, but it delayed electrification. In Finland, economic, cultural and geopolitical factors, by contrast, hampered invention much more than electrification.

The early start and development of electrification in Finland cannot be explained by the high levels of technical education or qualified scientific expertise. Although the rate of literacy was very high in the country, technological research and instruction took place on a very small scale. Only after 1911 was it possible to take the degree of graduate engineer in electrical technology at the new Helsinki University of Technology. In many other European countries, technical education was much better organized, for example, in 1910, Germany had eleven universities of technology, while Austria-Hungary and Russia both had seven. In Sweden, it was possible to take the electrical engineer's degree in two institutions.

Direct foreign investments in power plants, transmission lines, distribution utilities and energy-intensive industries have considerably promoted the development of electricity output in many countries. Although direct foreign investments were also made in Finland, they were far less extensive and less significant than the foreign involvement in Norway or Eastern Europe. From the turn of the century, transnational companies founded their subsidiaries to sell their electrical equipment in Finland. The importation of tangible products was a pivotal vehicle of technology transfer. By contrast, direct foreign investment in manufacturing products of electrical engineering was very modest. In the early twentieth century, the German transnational AEG took over four urban electricity supply utilities in Finland, but between 1918 and 1936 it sold them to municipal governments. From the

1940s to the late 1970s, the entire electricity supply sector and most of the electrical engineering companies were in the hands of Finnish owners. The role of transnational companies remained dominant only in the importation of electrical equipment, although a versatile electrical engineering industry grew up in Finland.

In summing up the results of the thesis, we can concentrate on the factors which promoted electrification in Finland. The brisk pace of development can primarily be attributed to five causes.

First, although the country had a rather narrow choice of indigenous natural resources, some of them, viz. hydropower, timber, and peat, were appropriate for power generation. Nevertheless, Finland's sources of indigenous energy were in no way comparable to those of Norway or Sweden, which – in terms of hydropower resources – have benefitted from the extraordinary gifts of nature. The generating capacity of Finland's technically exploitable hydropower resources were estimated in the mid-1960s to be only a third of Italy's, Yugoslavia's or Spain's potential and approximately the same as the resources of Romania or Greece. Measured in per capita terms, Finland, however, was in a somewhat better position than those countries.

During its initial phase, Finnish electrification in the nineteenth century was not based on the country's 'white coal'. Hydropower, however, became an important energy source for electricity generation only after the turn of the century, and the steep rise of output in interwar and early post-World War II Finland was primarily based on the extensive utilization of hydropower. In the early twentieth century, contemporaries already observed that countries with considerable hydropower resources tended to have more electricity to consume than other countries.

Finland has always been dependent on the continuous importation of foreign technology, but in terms of primary energy, the self-sufficiency of its electricity generation remained very high for a long time. Up to the late 1950s, over 90 % of electricity was generated by means of indigenous primary energy. During the following decade, the country's economically exploitable hydropower resources and wood wastes of the forest industries became almost fully utilized. The growth of electricity demand could no longer be met by means of indigenous primary energy. Therefore, the rate of self-sufficiency declined to about 50 %, where it remained up to the introduction of nuclear power in 1977.

Second, between 1890 and 1977 Finland's gross domestic product at constant prices grew on average 3.3 % per annum and the output of industrial production 5.0 % p.a. The country was capable of financing the heavy costs of power plants, long transmission lines, distribution networks and electricity consuming equipment by producing and exporting manufactured products by means of indigenous natural resources. Finland was very fortunate, because both world demand for its staple exports – sawn timber, pulp, board an paper – and its terms of trade developed favourably in the long run.

Since the rate of industrialization was fairly swift, it induced extensive investments in the production capacity. When building new factories, opportunities to introduce up-to-date technology were many and the most rapidly growing industries, such as wood-processing, were electricity-intensive. Together the above mentioned factors provided electrification with a beneficial economic basis.

Third, there was also another reason why Finland took advantage of its earlier backwardness. Because the industrialization of the country started only in the last third of the century, electricity faced very few competing technologies, such as the light and power provided by gas utilities. In Finland, there were only three urban gas utilities – in Helsinki, Turku and Viipuri. In the early 1920s, their number was, by contrast, 17 in Norway and 37 in Sweden. Electricity was thus granted a lot of technological Lebensraum.

Fourth, a crucial contextual factor was that the Finnish society of the late nineteenth centruy had a rather positive attitude toward industrialization and the adoption of innovations. The Finns were psychologically prepared to apply new technology which they accepted fairly unanimously as supporting their national aspirations. Consequently, electrification was backed by a favourable social-psychological and political support network.

Fifth, owing to reasonably good basic education standards and a mental preparedness to adopt new innovations, the Finns developed into eager, entrepreneural conveyers of foreign electrical technology. They preferred to use nationals primarily as carriers of technology and apply self-controlled mechanisms in the transfer process. This interesting feature of Finnish electrification seems to conflict with the conventional wisdom about the country carrying an image as a poor, agrarian periphery and a latecomer to industrialization. Another striking feature is that although Finland relied mainly on other transfer channels than direct foreign investments, it thrived. This fact sharply contradicts those theories which highlight the decisive role of transnational companies.

Finally, we could say that there was societal demand for electrical technology in Finland. This need was fulfilled by a relative efficient transfer of foreign technology and its rational application to local conditions. Meanwhile, the rapid growth of the Finnish economy and the very energy-intensive structure of the manufacturing industry constituted favourable economic preconditions for the transfer of electrical technology into the country. Although Finnish society in general was very selective in choosing transfer mechanisms of technology, it worked spurringly and in co-ordination with those transfer channels which were accepted. The success in the electrification of Finland cannot be ascribed to the pathbreaking indigenous inventions but to the entrepreneurial and resolute social engineering of technology transfer.

In an historical perspective, the lesson of the Finnish experience is that a self-controlled transfer of technology coupled with favourable economic development is not an impossible option for small, less developed countries. In general, it appears that most of technologies required by less developed countries can be, and indeed have been, introduced equally rapidly whatever the predominant transfer mechanism involved.

REFERENCE

This paper reports the results of my thesis *The Electrification of Finland, 1877-1977. The Transfer of a New Technology into a Late Industrialising Economy,* The London School of Economics and Political Science, The University of London (September, 1988).

WAGE DETERMINATION THEORY AND THE FIVE-DOLLAR DAY AT FORD : A DETAILED EXAMINATION

DANIEL MARTIN GORODETSKY RAFF

This thesis examines the Ford Motor Company's famous doubling of its minimum production wages to five dollars a day in 1914 in the light of current theories of wage determination. The event is one of the most famous moments in the history of American industrial labour markets. It followed closely a watershed moment in the history of American industrial production methods. Yet it has never been investigated with the methods of modern labour economics, and the significance of the production innovations for the firm's and the industry's employment practices has never been systematically investigated. Indeed, the history of the innovations' diffusion has remained unwritten. The thesis pursues these several tasks.

The central question, suggested by the efficiency wage literature, is whether the company's action could possibly have been a profit-maximizing policy. The answer to this question in terms of brute facts proves to be 'yes'. Since the wage offered can be shown to be greatly in excess of the opportunity cost of labour, this raises the further and intriguing question of the means by which paying such high wages could work to maximize profits. This second question has been debated implicitly by several generations of methodologically traditional historians. I frame it explicitly in terms of the recent economic theories (showing, in passing, how each lies behind one of the lines of traditional analysis) and address it on the basis of archival and other contemporary sources. The models enable me to lay out well-defined alternative explanations and to confront them with data that might, in principle, refute them. This procedure enables me to come to a sharp-edged conclusion about why the company undertook the policy : the data are strongly inconsistent with most of the explanations but they strongly support another. The particular form this company's welfare programs took fits in neatly with the other explanation.

I can summarize the negative conclusions more carefully as

follows. The high wage did not represent a compensating differential for those actually employed in the plant : at that wage there was in fact an excess supply of labour. Profits did indeed go up. But consideration of the plant's technology and recent changes in its production process suggests that none of the three most well-known efficiency wage theories – neoclassical models of the effects of turnover costs, adverse selection, and moral hazard – gives a plausible account of the source of the productivity growth. None, therefore, could be plausible central motive for raising wages so much.

To begin at the beginning, it is implausible that this huge rise in compensation represented the workings of supply and demand in the labour market. The country in general and the Mid-west in particular – both its rural and its industrial parts – were sliding into a depression. Poor relief in Detroit was at its highest levels in many years. Immense queues, on many days numbering as many twelve thousand and more, formed outside the Ford factory. These job-seekers were prepared to wait all night during a Great Lakes winter. Fire hoses could drive them away, but only for long enough for a change into dry clothes. It seems inescapable that Ford jobs were thought to offer surplus at the quoted wage.

Was the company just giving away its money? The contrary economist thinks immediately of the so-called efficiency wage theories surveyed by Yellin in the 1984 *AEA Papers and Proceedings.* Three of the theories she discusses are quite familiar to economists : training and other turnover costs, adverse selection, and moral hazard. But in the context of the changes we know to have been going on in the Ford production process at the time, changes being replicated nowhere else in the industry, none of these theories seems a plausible central explanation of the intra-industry pattern.

The thrust of the technological changes was to radically routinize all but a handful of the jobs at Ford. Workforce skills that were still crucial for producing autos elsewhere became progressively irrelevant to making cars at Ford : Ford engineers built the skills into single-purpose machine tools making strictly interchangeable parts instead. Since no-one was being employed in skilled fitting tasks whose timing was difficult to forecast, the pace of work throughout the factory became subject to centralized managerial control to a quite unprecedented degree. Even the jobs which were not strictly speaking on the assembly lines became driven by the line's rhythms.

Ford had dramatically heavy turnover in the period leading up to the five-dollar day, including one twelve-month period with a rate of 412 %. But deskilling had been going on fast enough and long enough that this was not necessarily very costly in terms of wasted training. Documents in the Ford Archives permit crude calculations of these costs. At the most resolutely optimistic, one cannot place them above 30 % of the profit-share.

Since the point of all this technical change was to allow essentially unskilled workmen to do the production work, adverse selection explanations appear to be irrelevant. Analysis of the tasks reveals that there were no unobservable but intrinsic skills or productivity attributes in the sense those models presume : by and large, the work was either machine-minding or assembly-line operations. One might be tempted to argue that ability to tolerate the pace was such an attribute. But this ability could be observed essentially instantaneously, for reasons I discuss in the next paragraph. The cost to hiring a person who did not have much of it was essentially zero.

The most obviously promising approach is moral hazard : perhaps there were many opportunities for the exercise of discretion and so for shirking. The high wage might serve as incentive to refrain if there was some chance of getting caught, since the alternative employments were all much less well-paid. The difficulty with this concerns the ease of monitoring, which got cheaper and more efficient (in the sense that the monitoring mechanisms identified shirkers and replaced them much more incisively and swiftly than before) as a part of the technical change.

The factory building was innovative. Architectural history and building plans reveal a structure designed to admit a new style of automobile construction. This building was not a craftsman's workshop, with the chassis on sawhorses in the center of the room and the tools and parts around the perimeter of the room. Instead, the shop-floor was laid out systematically for a progressive flow of work product. When everyone was keeping pace the work flowed along smoothly. When someone was not keeping pace, work-in-process piled up at his station. The sightlines in the new-style space were clean and long, and work-in-progress piling up was quickly spotted. (One might, of course, shirk by doing a job incompletely rather than slowly. But neither company records nor trade sources offer any positive evidence at all of this. Perhaps the division of labour was so radical that even these sorts of discretion were obvious to the supervisor.) The problem of monitoring individual shirking was thus getting less rather than more severe; and though the costs of the shirking were on the increase – more pieces going by each worker in each time unit – the speed with which shirkers could be caught and replaced was rising extremely quickly. Reports in the engineering and management press of the day suggest there was not in fact much scope for shirking. And ratios of supervisory staff of production workers seem to have been sharply on the rise.

On the other hand, the company's means of dealing with shirkers, however effective for isolated individuals, would have been very much less efficient in dealing with groups. These might be easy to identify; but swooping down on them, plucking them out of the circuit, and instantaneously replacing them with another group that knew exactly what to do would have been another matter entirely given that there were many fewer supervisers than jobs.

In the abstract, then, the possibility of collective action raises the question of work norms and the source of management's confidence that it could simply come in each day and unilaterally decide on the speed of the line. More concretely, it raises the specter of the sit-down strike. This was a company whose capital stock was to a first approximation completely dedicated to making black Model T Fords. The handsome stream of profits were rents to co-ordination involving the use of these machines. Collective action which interfered with that was a direct threat to the rents.

Such collective action was very much in the air in Detroit, Michigan in this period. I document the claim that it would have been on the minds of the relevant actors here, workers, managers, and owners, and then make in detail the claim that Ford's (expected-)profit-maximizing strategy was precisely the rent-sharing approach of buying the peace. The five-dollar day scheme began just after it became clear the company could do final assembly via a pace-controlled line and so would want to co-ordinate all work to those line's demands. Production would then become integrated to an unprecedented degree. Ford was a very profitable company, and its owners could see that through these developments it was in the process of becoming more so. I argue that the company decided to pay the handsome wage to such a large fraction of its employees because a very large fraction of its employees worked on the shop-floor. It was those on the shop-floor who could interfere with the action of the great machine. The idiosyncrasies of the Ford welfare capitalism programs are precisely what one would expect from an employer for whom it was unusually important for these reasons to buy the peace.

I argue that Ford was alone in his industry in paying such wages and implementing such welfare programs when he introduced the policies because he was alone in making automobiles in this way. This view has been explicitly and implicitly advanced before, though on the basis of crude output figures rather than of any careful analysis of the production process itself. I analyze the deep ambiguities ignored by such an approach and illustrate my points with calculations derived from archival data about shop-floor reorganization, production, and costs taken from another contemporary manufacturer who was demonstrably not implementing the Ford system. I argue Ford's uniqueness instead on the basis of articles in contemporary trade journals about shop practice in the industry, investment patterns and new facilities at other firms. I also rely on such minutes and production and cost data from other contemporary firms as have survived. (Such records survive from several firms. Each of these bodies of materials sheds interesting light in a number of ways.)

This picture of compensation/motivation policies and the production process in January 1914 does raise the question of what happened in the five-dollar day's aftermath. News articles soon brought the Highland Park plant and its methods great prominence. My argument strongly implies that as the production strategy and technology diffused across the industry, so too would (most notably) the relatively high wages. There is no evidence of sympathetic wage rises in the five-dollar day's immediate (and even medium-term) aftermath. That suggests that even in the medium term (i.e. into the years of World War I) the Ford production process went substantially unimitated. Could it really be that such a profitable innovation did not diffuse swiftly? I also investigate this question.

The answer does appear to be 'yes'. Even cursory research reveals that moving assembly lines were in place in a number of other firms circa 1916. Articles in the trade press suggest these were responsible for Ford-style quantity production, generally constituted mass production methods in themselves, and offered all Ford's opportunities for centralized control over pace. But one can identify excellent reasons to doubt each of these claims. There is very considerable evidence to suggest the conveyors were being used largely as labour-saving devices rather than as devices of co-ordination and control. To the extent they did have the latter use, such evidence as I have seen suggests control was being exerted only over the final assembly of completed sub-units. I have found no traces of routinization reaching deep into the production process, into the production of components, as at Ford. It is worth bearing in mind that at no stage were a majority of the Ford workers standing by the side of a line. Most fed or otherwise tended machines.

The point is that the central innovation at Ford was not the conveyor belt. The ideas that really made Ford production possible were progressive assembly and the American System of interchangeable parts production. Progressive assembly and some conveyors were clearly compatible whether or not the parts required fitting. Even when many parts required quite considerable fitting, the two combined would expand production considerably. Parts moved more efficiently. Men did not wander. But men wandering the shopfloor evading work is only the grossest form of shirking. The real source of the huge Ford output lay in the American system, in doing away with direct production tasks that required discretion. Ford did this by large-scale investment in the requisite machines and tools. And that does not seem to have been common until the early 1920s.

The history of the diffusion of Ford's production idea – as against the mere diffusion of some of the machines – appears, then, to be a distinctly post-World War I phenomenon. I am exploring the details of that and its implications for compensation, other motivation systems, and the history of welfare capitalism in current research.

TRANSITION IN INDIAN HANDLOOM WEAVING, 1900-1939

TIRTHANKAR ROY

THE PROBLEM

Handicrafts occupy a prominent place in the literature on Indian industrialization and in Indian macroeconomics generally. Indeed it is a measure of their considerable and continuing importance in the national economy. Yet, the empirical basis for making any generalization on this sector remains extremely weak so that hypotheses about them often have the character of assertions.

The present study addresses itself to this problem and is primarily an attempt to construct a systematic data-base for handloom weaving with a view to identifying the questions that can be answered with the available information. This apparently neutral task, however, involves a shift in focus: from the extensively debated issue in growth and decay, 'deindustrialization' and 'survival' of the textile crafts, to aspects of structural change – production relations, product composition, technology and location. This shift in focus follows on the notion that handlooms were an industry which did not, in the long run, simply survive, but was going through a complex process of transformation. The existence of a mechanized industry induced adaptations and not a passive decay in the textile handicrafts. This idea is both a conclusion and a prior framework for the study and guides our collection and classification of information throughout.

The justification for a detailed study of handloom growth process and of a structural change in particular derive not only negatively from a gap, but also from categorical questions that can be asked about Indian industries. These questions can be grouped under three heads: small scale manufacturing in contemporary India, textiles and textile history, and historiography of industrialization. In relation to the present study these questions form a background rather than the direct subject matter, but they do strengthen our case for a shift in focus.

Recent statistics on household and unregistered manufacturing suggest stagnation in employment and slowly rising value added, though the level of the latter is believed to be underestimated. Disaggregation produces a more complex picture. The textiles case, for instance, suggests that a stagnation in overall scale can be consistent with the presence of dynamic and successful segments within, small powerlooms and technologically equipped handloom factories. If the textiles case is even partially generalizable, what seems to have happened within a segment of the small scale industries is not an absolute decline but a polarization.

The coexistence of modern and traditional technologies in textiles has proved relatively stable historically. What are the conditions for this coexistence? What characteristics has the traditional sector's growth process assumed under these conditions? Has the coexistence been secured by means of a passive survival or of dynamic adjustments? If the latter, then what constituted these adjustments?

Recent industrial history has implicitly identified itself with large scale industries. This may imply (a) attributing a certain changelessness to the crafts while modern industries are believed to form the dynamic element, a notion the findings of the thesis reject, and (b) perceiving an opposition between the two sectors, for instance through competition between mill and handloom cloths. On empirical grounds 'competiton' can be questioned. But there is also a methodological point involved. Surely there can be many common grounds between the two histories and common processes to which both were subject? Consider the reversal in handloom growth trend, from absolute decline in late-nineteenth century to accelerated growth in the twentieth (Chapter 1). If deindustrialization is given the sense Rakshit (1982) had attributed it, a reflection of insufficient food surplus, then the reversal could equally reflect accumulation in agriculture, reduced fluctuations, smaller inventory and exports. But this is at once a precondition for industrialization in general, obliterating the distinction between small and large.

Lastly, a study of Indian textile crafts can contribute to a neglected theme in comparative history. Specifically, the Indian transition can be seen as an instance of a more generalized model that occurs in major Asian weaving regions, the Middle East, Java, north and central China. In each case handlooms survived the entry of machine-woven cloth not by immiserising but by adapting themselves. The movement was externally induced in a sense transition in eighteenth century rural Europe, with which the Asian case bears similarity in detail, was not. But also, in each region of Asia a different effect followed because the social and economic bases of craft production were not the same. For instance, the peasant household weaver was common in China but comparatively rare in India. Detailed case studies of the sort the thesis attempts to do can lead to a typology of evolution in crafts.

SUMMARY OF MAIN ARGUMENTS

Deindustrialization, both the fact and the abstract process, is a convenient starting point, for our own attempt at describing the handloom industry can proceed by contrast. For the third and possibly the second quarter of the nineteenth century a significant and absolute fall in textile employment is well-established through the works of Bagchi (1967) and Twomey (1983). But it is equally clear that since about 1900 handloom production was rising at a steady pace (Chapter 1). To explore the characteristics of this reversal and conditions for it to happen constitutes an objective of this study.

The empirical question, however, is of limited importance. What is crucial are the methodological implications. For deindustrialization is also a theory, of what would happen to traditional manufactures when a country opens up. General conceptions of handloom evolution which has decay as its focus tend to be associated with two characteristics. Firstly, concern with industry size dominate over questions of structure. Secondly, static notions are developed to account for survival where the fact of survival is acknowledged. The best-known instance of the latter is, of course, the idea that households survived by exploiting family labour, or the industry survived precisely by ruling out structural change.

The present study rejects both positions on two grounds. Firstly, we have to account for a large number of facts which do not bear on decay or growth. The extent and richness of this information render industry size a narrow and by itself uninteresting point to debate. And secondly, any passive survival thesis can be shown to be empirically weak for the period in question. Historical sources suggest, on the contrary, capital accumulation within the crafts.

The worth of an alternative framework, however, would depend not only on the range of questions it can generate, but also on its specific empirical content. A more precise account of what we have meant by 'structural change' is, therefore, necessary. Four basic processes, all closely interrelated, are identified:

(1) Output composition – Reestimates of output show that the twentieth century reversal in trend was associated not as much with import substitution, as a straight reading might suggest, as with continuous diversification into high value-added, skill intensive and technologically complex products.

(2) Production relations – There was increasing inequality and polarization among producers resulting in what was frequently termed reduction of 'independent' weavers, independence conceived in terms of production decisions and choice of markets, to 'dependence'. Two basic forms of dependence can be distinguished, contract for sale of products tied to a merchant and contract for sale of labour tied to a large producer. The best example of the latter was wage-work in the rapidly growing handloom factories of southern and western India. The status of the household as a producing unit was correspondingly eroded.

(3) Location – Town weaving was both more complex and more progressive than rural. This was reflected in urbanization of handlooms.

(4) Technology – Preference for technical options that displaced (family) labour in pre-weaving processes reflected and reinforced weakening of the household.

Description of structural processes would not be complete without reference to regional differences in their expression. These differences had a systematic component. By assembling a set of criteria the study distinguishes between two macro-regions, to be referred as the 'south' and the 'north'. Broadly, south includes the handloom complexes of Bombay-Deccan, Hyderabad, coastal Andhra, Tamil Nadu and Malabar, and the north includes the complexes of Punjab, eastern UP, Bihar, Orissa and Bengal. Clearly, the terms do not strictly refer to geographical areas. The distinction is also not categorical. It does capture a basic feature of the industry but is subject to modification whenever exceptional facts appear and differences within macro-regions are encountered.

Southern weaving, the study argues, was more progressive than the northern. In relations of production, the tendency towards wage-labour and factories was more pronounced here and large producers formed a powerful class. Proletarianization was aided by external circumstances, such as immigration of weavers from Rayalaseema to the handloom towns of Deccan. In the largely rural weaving of the north, in contrast, the dominant capitalist was a nonproducer, a yarn-merchant or moneylender. Increasing dependence represented an intensification of merchant-producer difference, just as in the south it represented differentiation among producers. As in the south, large producers appeared in the north too, but were in relations of conflict or collaboration with merchants.

Structural processes derived partly from characteristics peculiar to the crafts. But a full conception must situate them within the context in which the crafts functioned. The principal element in this was, of course, the presence of mill-made cloth. Broadly, two perceptions of this coexistence are available to us. In one, handloom and machine cloth participated in a common 'world market'. In the other, each created a distinct market for itself protected by product differentiation and preference rigidities. Taken in isolation either hypothesis denies the necessity of structural change. The implications are different when both are combined.

Direct competition was indeed significant in certain segments of the market, mainly plain cotton fabrics of coarse-medium counts. But within a vast range of product involving finer yarn and special skills possibilities of product differentiation were unlimited. These 'discrete' markets, however, constituted a field the boundaries of which were constantly shifting because preferences could change and machines imitated handloom cloth, or vice versa. They represented regimes of potential or, to use a contemporary term, 'indirect' competition.

Partial, as opposed to total, competition intensified differentiation among producers. Only those already better-placed could diversify and survive. But the more vulnerable faced stiffer barriers to entry and could only offer their labour. Similarly, potential competition increased uncertainty and made risk-bearing a costlier process, with the same effect.

Long-run diversifications can be interpreted as a search for areas relatively free from mill competition. Roughly two sort of product-structural adjustments followed, a static sort in which shifts in products did not involve changes in organization or technology, e.g. from fine to coarse weaving or the reverse, and a dynamic kind which necessitated changes in the technoeconomic bases. Static adjustments seem to have characterized the latter part of the nineteenth century while dynamic adjustments were more common in the twentieth. Like the north-south distinction, the static-dynamic adjustment is no more than a conceptual tool and allows for exceptions. But to the extent they were present, market-induced changes converged into and strenghtened the differentiation processes already at work.

CHAPTER OUTLINE

Chapters 1 and 2 attempt a statistical survey, the first concerned with trend while the second with short run output estimates. The statistical review reconstructs the picture of an industry in transition, gradually overcoming short run constraints and expanding steadily. Over the expansion phase production depended more on income than on relative prices, contradicting the notion that direct competition consituted an important element in handloom experience. Growth was associated with polarization between producers and with technological changes of a sort that reinforced the former.

Chapter 3 classifies the relational changes experienced, and Chapter 4 analyses the various options for product structural adjustments that were allowed by the market, that is, by the prevailing bases of market sharing in textiles. Chapter 5 explores the regional dimension. This involves two distinct tasks : to clearly define the macro-regions, and to develop a distinction between 'town' and 'country' production systems which suggests a correlation between urbanization of weaving and the technical or relational changes a region would experience.

Chapter 6 identifies feasible technical options and relates revealed choices to the abstract benefit-cost ranking. In Chapter 7 the scope of state intervention is studied more in terms of evolution of concepts than of assessment of policies. The review suggests a reorientation, from state aid conceived statically as protecting the weak from exploitation by capitalists towards a more pragmatic and collaborationist policy addressed to specific problems related to technology and marketing.

A concluding section studies continuity and change in structural processes under dominant state intervention after 1947. A major intent of this section is to suggest directions in which data bases on contemporary handlooms could develop.

REFERENCES

A.K. Bagchi, 'Deindustrialization in India in the nineteenth century: Some theoretical implications', *Journal of Development Studies,* 12 (1976), 135-164.

M. Rakshit, *The Labour Surplus Economy* (New Delhi, 1982).

M.J. Twomey, 'Employment in nineteenth century India textiles', *Explorations in Economic History,* 20 (1983), 37-57.

THE DYNAMICS AND THE DISMANTLING OF THE RURAL STRUCTURE OF INCOME AND SURVIVAL THE 'KEMPEN' (CAMPINE) AREA OF ANTWERP BETWEEN 1750 AND 1910

ERIC VANHAUTE

Rural economy research is by definition integrated; the historian is at an intersection where various approaches and problems meet. This implies that well defined questions and an appropriate methodology are required.

THE PROBLEMS

Up to the present, rural history predominantly implies the investigation of the organization of the agrarian economy or of the influence of external developments. By focussing attention on the dynamics and the dismantling of internal strategies of income and survival, we look at it from another angle.

Therefore, integrated socio-economic micro-investigation differs fundamentally from agrarian history (no overall picture of the rural society), from the socio-political approach (which often neglects investigation into the material basis of survival), and from regional research that starts out from a macro-angle approach (appropriate for the reconstruction of the economic *conjoncture,* but not for the analysis of the shifts in the structure of income). Consequently, we argue for an approach that is, at the same time, narrow and broad. First of all, the primary attention has to go to the internal composition of income, but second, rural income has to be interpreted in its broadest sense as well.

In order to ask the relevant questions and to interpret the observed movements, we start from an interpretation-scheme with two components. The first concerns the most important social development that marks the period that is studied, namely the growing influence of capitalist production methods on the socio-economic organization and the resultant process of massive proletarianization. Changes in socio-economic structures (such as transformations in relations of labour, of ownership of property, of power and of surplus-extraction) are viewed in this light. Second, we wish to point out the peculiarity of 'peasant economies'. The starting point is that the classic 'market'-theory is unsuitable for defining the non-capitalistic organization of the countryside. Its central characteristics are the dynamics, the flexibility, the competitivity, and the resistance against increasing commercialization. Since we do not start from an opposition between traditional and modern, between rigid and dynamic, between internal and external, but from a dialectic relationship between these two poles, we oppose the regulated, linear, and often a-historical concepts of modernization.

From this general approach, we distill three basic theses. First, the process of desintegration in the country as a result of the dismantling of internal survival circuits is not due to rigidity or inertia of country life. It is, rather, structurally linked to the development of a capitalistic mode of production. Second, the traditional rural economic structure which sustained rural life until the beginning of the 20th century, was basically resilient and dynamic. Finally, in order to study a rural community, it is essential to start from the specific structure of income and survival. Working with a 'macro-lens' inevitably leads to reduced concepts.

The actual research deals with the country east of the harbour city of Antwerp, the Kempen (or Campine area) of Antwerp, and covers the period between 1750 and 1910. In order to test our hypotheses, we start out from two sets of questions.

First, what is the composition of the socio-economic substructure of income? What elements account for the coherence and the resilience? At what moment does the process of undermining start in earnest?

Second, what is the typical social organization of this region and what are the results of the process of dismantling that was mentioned above? Can they be translated in terms of proletarianization, polarization, and impoverishment?

METHODOLOGY

Integrated research bears upon two factors. First of all, differernt lines of approach are combined to form an overall picture. Moreover, the study relies on basic cross-sections, composed by gathering information per household from different socio-economic and demographic censuses. This procedure is an improvement on two methods that dominate socio-economic micro-research. The first of these methods concerns the measuring of the active population and of economic activity. Only a few censuses give an exhaustive enumeration of professions. Moreover, a (defective) reconstruction of the supply of, and the demand for, labour by the exclusion of informal and non-commercial circuits of income yields only a very incomplete picture of the socio-economic organization in a rural community.

To counter this criticism, a model of social stratification is often built in. However, a non-integrated, static, regulated and very hierarchic approach has proved too vulnerable (dependent on one source, e.g., fiscal lists) and unreliable. Summarizing, we start from a carefully selected line of inquiry into rural income in its broadest sense, which requires a wide approach in which the various points of view are combined.

The research concerns the Kempen of Antwerp, a poor, sandy region with many small farms and little agrarian wage labour (70 % of the farms are smaller than 2 hectares) and is restricted to three villages, each representing a specific region : Dessel in the canton of Arendonk (intensive proto-industry on the basis of wool until 1850), Rijkevorsel in the canton of Hoogstraten (a closed region untill the end of the 19th century, from then onwards brickworks), Walem in the region of Duffel and Malines (a more accessible region on the Campine border between Antwerp and Malines with market oriented cultivation of potatoes and vegetables from the last quarter of the 19th century onwards).

By taking into account such a long period, between 1750 and 1910, it is possible to trace the evolution of these rural communities from the period before the major economic, social and political changes until the eve of the vanishing of the 'old world'.

MAIN CONCLUSIONS

The results of this research can be divided into four levels: the structure of property holding, the structure of labour, the structure of income, and the structure of survival. To conclude, we show the consequenses of the observed evolutions on the social configuration of the villages.

1. Organization of property holding: a process of expropriation

Between 1750 and 1910, a double evolution concerning the ownership of real estate took place: a growing importance of non-resident owners of the Campine land (7 to 15 % in 1750 to 40 % of the land in 1910), and an increase in the number of households without land (5 to 10 % in 1750, 25 % (Dessel) to 60 % (Rijkevorsel) in 1910). The number of families that owned more than 2 ha (the absolute minimum for a subsistence farm) diminished from 60 to 65 % in 1750 to about 20 % at the beginning of the 20th century. Greater pressure on the leasing market of real estate had firmly raised the price of land: in real terms (rye and daily wages), it tripled or quadrupled during the period under consideration.

2. Organization of labour: an increasing lack of balance between supply and demand

A comparison between the demand in the economic sectors – expressed in the number of active workers (participation of labour), as well as in the number of man years (input of labour) – and the supply shows increasing tension on the rural labour market from the second half of the 19th century onwards. An unequal distribution of tasks makes a (temporary) surplus of labour inherent to an agricultural economy (which accounts for the ease with which proto-industrial activity absorbs this surplus), but the greater supply of workers form the end of the 19th century onwards is only partly compensated for by a process of intensification in agriculture and by new possibilities in the secondary and tertiary sector. The consequence of this is twofold: a growing surplus of labour in the primary sector (division of activities without increasing the total input) and in a variety of related, underlying, informal circuits, and a shrinking of the (agrarian and non-agrarian) independent status of exploitation (in 1910, 40 to 60 % of the active population).

3. Organization of income: an increasing instability

The disruption of concord between labour and business is translated into a more dependent income position. Two parameters illustrate this. Between 1750 and 1910, the relative number of households that were able to manage on agricultural activities was cut by half (60 to 30 %), whereas the number of families dependent on hired labour grew larger and larger (from 15-25 % to 60-70 %). The consequence of this was that on the one hand combined income became more and more important (earnings from various sectors within the household : 35-40 % of the households in 1750 to 65-70 % in 1910) and that on the other hand the loss of the local population's control of its own position of survival was accelerated. Wage labour was mostly a non full-time occupation (seasonal unemployment, e.g., in the brickworks) and the earnings remained very low until a few years before 'The Great War' (not enough to feed one's family). It was only after 1900 that the level of the middle of the 18th century was reached again and exceeded. Finally, we must take into consideration the greater burden of surplus-extraction (especially in favour of private social groups by way of rental and leasing; the tax-burden remained very low in the 19th century) : up to one third of the gross yield of one hectare of rye in the Campine villages and more than 75 % (high rents) in the Malines community, Walem.

A fast growing group of the population became dependent on precarious and uncertain strategies of income pooling towards the end of the 19th century. The fact that a rural exodus failed to occur can be explained by the flexibility of the rural organization of survival.

4. Strategies of survival: dynamics and dismantling

Dynamics.

The rural network of survival is a combination of formal and informal circuits of labour, income, and services. Paramount is the combined and global domestic income: agriculture, the two other 'formal' economic sectors, 'cheap' circuits of goods and services, common usage, activities in the semi-illegal domain (such as smuggling, wood-gathering, ...) etc. As long as the whole of the stabilizing bases is not affected, the rural income structure is characterized by great elasticity. Again, we refer to the ease with which domestic industry is combined with agricultural activities. This is in shrill contrast to the problematic connection between relative surplus-population in the country and the proletariat in the urban factories. The agricultural activity is mainly responsible for the dynamics and the resilience of the rural socio-economic structures. First of all, it guarantees regional self-supply (which became more and more solid in the course of the 19th century). This is due to important quantitative (acreage) and qualitative (productivity) improvements during the second and third quarters of the 19th century and is a consequence of internal activities (reclamations, production of manure, etc.). Apart from this, the larger part of Campine families continued to rely on at least a few acres of land (+ 90 % of the households) and, to a lesser degree, on one or more heads of livestock (stable at 70-75 %, thanks to an increasing breeding of pigs and goats).

Dismantling.

This structure of income specific for a rural community is the primary stabilizing element in the survival network. Only when, from the end of the 19th century onwards, various bases were permanently undermined (property holding, independent agricultural industry, common usage, possibilities of income – like domestic industry – adapted to an agrarian community) can we speak of a rupture in rural history. This development was intensified by changes in the demographic pattern. Owing to the looser ties with the soil and exploitation, less restrictive nuptial behaviour developed, but without affecting high fertility. The consequences of this were high birth rates (40 to 45 per thousand after 1900) and a broadening basis of the population pyramid ('non-active' population).

We repeat that, although a growing part of the rural population became mobile, a massive exodus failed to occur. Because many elements of the 'cheap' countryside remained functional (specific structuring of price and income) and because the possibilities of commuting and temporary migration became greater (infrastructure, public transport, bicycle), permanent emigration remained the last step, taken only when other possibilities had been exhausted.

5. A process of social subsidence

The micro-research (integrated cross-sections) enables us to determine the quantitative extent and the qualitative characteristics of the social substratum. The term refers to that section of the population that is either fully proletarianized (no real estate property, little agrarian capital (i.e. no live-stock), and no independent labour status), or that, owing to various strategies of combination of income, balances on the verge of the rural mechanism of survival.

Table : Extent of the social substratum (% of total population)

	Dessel	Rijkevorsel	Walem
1750	20-25 %	20-25 %	30-35 %
1800	25-30 %	25-30 %	50-55 %
1850	30-35 %	30-35 %	50-55 %
1910	40-45 %	45-50 %	60-65 %

It is obvious that we are dealing with a process of proletarianization and polarization (the superstratum does not shrink). However, we have to be more cautious with the term pauperization. When it is associated with a crisis of subsistence or with hunger, this concept is not appropriate. However, the use of it as a synonym for the increasing instability of income allows us to bring in the notion of a process of impoverishment as well. In doing this we indicate that both interpretations are not contradictory : a better economic output (with a possible input of 'cash-crops' such as the growing of potatoes and vegetables) and social polarization.

A growing number of households without or with little property, greater pressure on the labour market and an increasing hidden supply of labour in the agricultural sector and related informal circuits, more uncertain strategies of income (income pooling), the undermining of stabilizing bases in the structure of survival; all these factors explain the process of social subsidence which continued until the first decade of the 20th century. We must remember two important characteristics in order to interpret correctly the evolutions mentioned above.

First, there is the striking continuity and resilience of internal rural structures. We can only speak of a rupture from the end of the 19th century onwards, but even then the existing rural organization prevented a rural exodus.

Second, we encounter similar changes in the three studied regions, although with different periodicity and intensity. This indicates again that there was no link between processes of social destabilization and desintegration and the supposed inertia in the country, but rather there was one between the above-mentioned developments and the progressive capitalistic organization which had a growing impact on every subdivision of society.

The formation of a relative surplus-population and processes of economic and social reallocation must be seen in this light. In opposing ourselves to a monocausal explanation (demography, soil, external integration, etc.) we also indicate that research with a socio-political focus cannot start from the opposition traditional-modern (emphasis on the continuity in internal structures of power; the integration in the catholic master-organization from the end of the 19th century onwards, also as a result of the vacuum left by the dismantling of the traditional survival structure). Furthermore, a continuous confrontation with socio-economic mechanisms of survival seems indispensible.

NOTES ON THE CONTRIBUTORS
(in alphabetical order)

DANIEL BARBEZAT

Was born in Johannesburg (South Africa) in 1960. He wrote his dissertation at the University of Illinois at Champaign and is currently employed by the Department of Economics at Amherst College (Massachusetts).

Address: Department of Economics – Amherst College, Amherst, MA 01002 (USA).

JAN BIELEMAN

Was born in Heino (the Netherlands) in 1949. He received his doctoral degree from the Agricultural University at Wageningen and is presently lecturing at the department of rural history at the same university.

Address: Vakgroep agrarische geschiedenis van de Landbouwuniversiteit van Wageningen – Hollandseweg 1, 6706 KN Wageningen (the Netherlands).

KRISTINE BRULAND

Was born in Oslo (Norway) in 1950. Having completed her doctoral dissertation at the University of Oxford, she is currently engaged as a research fellow at the Centre for Technology and Culture at the University of Oslo.

Address: Centre for Technology and Culture, University of Oslo – Forskningsparken, Gaustadalleen 21, 0371 Oslo 3 (Norway).

SALLY CLARK

Was born in 1958 in Baltimore, Maryland (USA). She received her doctoral degree at Brown University and is currently an Assistant Professor at the University of Texas.

Address: University of Texas, Department of History – Austin, Texas 78712 (USA).

PHILIPPE DESY

Was born in Anderlecht (Belgium) in 1957 and was awarded his doctorate by the Université Libre de Bruxelles. He is currently part-time assistant at this University and teaching at a secondary school in Brussels.

Address (home): rue Henri Vieuxtemps 35/3, B-1070 Brussels (Belgium).

RUTH DUPRÉ

Was born in Montréal (Canada) in 1952 and defended her thesis at the University of Toronto. She is now Assistant Professor at the Institut d'économie appliquée of the Ecole des Hautes Etudes Commerciales.

Address: Institut d'économie appliquée, Ecole des Hautes Etudes

Commerciales – 5255, avenue Decelles, Montréal, Quebec H3T 1V6 (Canada).

PIOTR FRANASZEK
Was born in Malbork (Poland) in 1955. He received his doctorate from the Jagiellonian University in Cracow. He is currently employed at the Department of Social and Economic History of this University.
Address : Jagiellonian University, Institute of History – Department of Social and Economic History, Ul. Golebia 13, Cracow (Poland).

ÉVA MÁRIA FÜLÖP
Was born in Tatabánya (Hungary) in 1953 and completed her doctoral studies at the Attila József University in Szeged. She is now working as a scientific secretary at the Hungarian Agricultural Museum.
Address : Hungarian Agricultural Museum – 1367 Budapest 5, P.O. Box 129, H-1367 (Hungaria).

PATRICK RICHARD GALLOWAY
Was born in New Jersey (USA) in 1949 and received his Ph.D. at the University of California, Berkeley. He is currently a research associate at the graduate group in demography of the same university.
Address : University of California, Graduate Group in Demography – 2232 Piedmont Avenue, Berkeley CA 94720 (USA).

BORIS GREKOV
Was born in Moscow (USSR) in 1950. He defended his thesis at the Institute of General History of the Academy of Sciences of the USSR. He is a scientific member of this Institute.
Address : Academy of Sciences of the USSR, Institute of General History – Moscow (USSR).

WILLEM JONGMAN
Was born in Zaandam (the Netherlands) in 1953. He completed his doctoral studies at the Rijksuniversiteit Leiden. Currently not affiliated.
Address (home) : Stroveer 268, 3032 GA Rotterdam (the Netherlands).

ANDREAS KIESELBACH
Was born in 1959 in Leipzig (German Democratic Republic). He defended his doctoral dissertation at the Hochschule für Verkehrswesen in Dresden. He is a researcher at the same institute.
Address : Hochschule für Verkehrswesen Friedrich List, Wirtschafts- und Verkehrsgeschichte – Postbox 103, Dresden 8072 (German Democratic Republic).

CEZARY KUKLO
Was born in Bialystok (Poland) in 1954. He obtained his doctoral degree from the University of Warsaw and is presently employed by the same university.

Address: Institute of History, University of Warsaw – 20 U. Swierkowa, 15328 Bialystok (Poland).

MONIQUE LAKROUM

Was born in Suresnes (France), in 1953. She wrote her doctoral thesis at the Université Paris VII and is now Professor at the Université de Reims.
Address: Université de Reims, Faculté des Sciences Humaines, Département d'Histoire – 57 Rue Pierre Taittinger, 51096 Reims cédex (France).

JAROSLAV LÁNIK

Was born in Svitavy (Czechoslovakia) in 1957. Having earned his doctorate at the Institute of Czechoslovak and World History of the Academy of Sciences, he now works there as a research assistant.
Address: CSAS – Vyšehradská 49, 128 26 Praha 2 (Czechoslovakia).

SERGEI LEBEDEV

Was born in Archangelsk (USSR) in 1956 and presented his doctoral thesis at the Leningrad branch of the Institute of USSR History. He is fellow of this Institute.
Address: Institute of USSR History, Academy of Sciences of the USSR – Petrozavodskaja ul. 7, 197110 Leningrad (USSR).

GONÇAL LÓPEZ NADAL

Was born in 1953 in Palma de Mallorca (Spain) and wrote his dissertation at the Universitat Autònoma de Barcelona. He is now lecturer in economic history at the Universitat de les Illes Balears.
Address: Universitat de les Illes Balears, Departament de Ciències Històriques i Teoria de les Arts, Facultat de Lletres – Carretera de Valldemossa, Km. 7I5, 07071 Palma de Mallorca (Spain).

CARLES MANERA

Was born in Palma de Mallorca (Spain) in 1957 and was awarded his doctorate by the University of Les Illes Balears. He is now Professor of Modern Economic History at this University.
Address: Universitat de les Illes Balears, Departament de Ciències Històriques i Teoria de les Arts, Facultat de Lletres – Carretera de Valldemossa, Km. 7I5, 07071 Palma de Mallorca (Spain).

MATS MORELL

Was born in 1955 in Lillhärad in Västmanland (Sweden) and defended his thesis at Uppsala University. He is a researcher *(forskarassistent)* at the Department of Economic History at the same University.
Address: Uppsala Universitet, Ekonomisk-historiska institutionen – HSC – Kyrkogårdsgatan 10, box 513, S/751 21 Uppsala (Sweden).

TIMO MYLLYNTAUS

Was born in Jyväskylä (Finland) in 1951. He received his Ph.D. degree from the London School of Economics and Political Science and is currently research fellow at the Department of Economic and Social History of the University of Helsinki.

Address: University of Helsinky, Department of Economic and Social History – Aleksanterinkatu 7, SF-00100 Helsinki (Finland).

ANDRZEJ POŚPIECH

Was born in 1952 in Warsaw (Poland). He earned his doctorate from the University of Warsaw and is presently affiliated with the Institute for the History of Material Culture of the Polish Academy of Sciences.

Address: Instytut Historii Kultury Materialnej PAN – 00/140 Warsaw, Ul. Swierczewskiego 105 (Poland).

DANIEL RAFF

Was born in Washington D.C. in 1951. He defended his doctoral thesis at the Massachusetts Institute of Technology. He is currently Assistant Professor of Business at the Harvard Graduate School of Business Administration.

Address: Harvard Graduate School of Business Administration – Soldiers Field, Boston MA 02163 (USA).

TIRTHANKAR ROY

Was born in Calcutta (India) in 1960, received a doctorate at the Jawaharlal Nehru University of New Delhi and is presently working as a researcher at the Gujarat Institute of Area Planning.

Address: Gujarat Institute of Area Planning – Sarkhej-Gandhinagar Highway, Gota/382 481, Ahmedabad Distr. Gujarat (India).

ERIK THOEN

Was born in 1953 (Belgium) and completed his doctoral studies at the State University of Ghent. He is presently research associate of the Belgian National Fund for Scientific Research.

Address: Rijksuniversiteit Gent, Seminarie voor Middeleeuwse Geschiedenis – Blandijnberg 2, 9000 Gent (Belgium).

ERIK VANHAUTE

Was born in Turnhout (Belgium) in 1959 and received his doctoral degree at the State University of Ghent. He is now senior research assistant of the Belgian National Fund for Scientific Research.

Address: Rijksuniversiteit Gent, Seminarie voor Nieuwste Geschiedenis – Blandijnberg 2, 9000 Gent (Belgium).

TENTH INTERNATIONAL
ECONOMIC HISTORY CONGRESS
PUBLICATIONS

General Editor: Erik AERTS

A **Debates and Controversies in Economic History**
Herman Van der Wee and Erik Aerts, editors

B-1 **Economic Effects of the French Revolutionary and Napoleonic Wars**
Erik Aerts and François Crouzet, editors

B-2 **Structures and Dynamics of Agricultural Exploitations: Ownership, Occupation, Investment, Credit, Markets**
Erik Aerts, Maurice Aymard, Juhan Kahk, Gilles Postel-Vinay and Richard Sutch, editors

B-3 **Economic and Demographic Development in Rice Producing Societies: Some Aspects of East Asian Economic History (1500-1900)**
Akira Hayami and Yoshihiro Tsubouchi, editors

B-4 **Economic Planning in the Post-1945 Period**
Erik Aerts and Alan S. Milward, editors

B-5 **Ethnic Minority Groups in Town and Countryside and Their Effects on Economic Development (1850-1940)**
Erik Aerts and Francis M.L. Thompson, editors

B-6 **Metropolitan Cities and Their Hinterlands in Early Modern Europe**
Erik Aerts and Peter Clark, editors

B-7 **Shipping and Trade (1750-1950)**
Lewis R. Fischer and Helge W. Nordvik, editors

B-8 Women in the Labour Force: Comparative Studies on Labour Market and Organization of Work since the 18th Century
Erik Aerts, Paul M.M. Klep, Jürgen Kocka and Marina Thorborg, editors

B-9 Unemployment and Underemployment in Historical Perspective
Erik Aerts and Barry Eichengreen, editors

B-10 Growth and Stagnation in the Mediterranean World in the 19th and 20th Centuries
Erik Aerts and Nuno Valério, editors

B-11 Models of Regional Economies in Antiquity and the Middle Ages to the 11th Century
Erik Aerts, Jean Andreau and Peter Ørsted, editors

B-12a Methodological Problems
Erik Aerts, Thomas Kuczynski and Vladimir Vinogradov, editors

B-12b Historical Information Systems
Rainer Metz, Eddy Van Cauwenberghe and Roel van der Voort, editors

B-13 Liberalism and Paternalism in the 19th Century
Erik Aerts, Claude Beaud and Jean Stengers, editors

B-14 Production, Marketing and Consumption of Alcoholic Beverages since the Late Middle Ages
Erik Aerts, Louis M. Cullen and Richard G. Wilson, editors

B-15 Textiles of the Low Countries in European Economic History
Erik Aerts and John H. Munro, editors

B-16 The Town as Regional Economic Centre in the Ancient Near East
Erik Aerts and Horst Klengel, editors

D Recent Doctoral Research in Economic History
Erik Aerts and Herman Van der Wee, editors

The organizers of the Leuven congress would like to express their gratitude to the following firms and public institutions whose generous help has made the publication of the proceedings possible.

ABB
Air Zaïre
Almanij
Association Suisse d'Histoire Economique et Sociale
Bank Brussel Lambert
Bank Brussel Lambert, Brugge
Bank Brussel Lambert, Leuven
Beaulieu
Belgische Arbeiderscoöperatie
Belgische Vereniging der Banken, Leuven
CERA Spaarbank
CMB
Cockerill Sambre
Commissariaat-Generaal voor de Internationale Samenwerking
De Vaderlandsche
De Volksverzekeringen
Dienst voor Internationale Betrekkingen, Vlaamse Gemeenschap
Ecoval
European Community
Francqui-Fonds
Gebroeders Van de Velde
Gemeentekrediet
Generale Bank, Brugge
Generale Bank, Leuven
Generale Maatschappij van België
Gevaert
Havenbedrijf Antwerpen
IBM Belgium
International Economic History Association
Janssen Pharmaceutica
J. Van Breda & Co
Katholieke Universiteit Leuven
Kempische Steenkoolmijnen
Kredietbank
Kredietbank, Brabant
Kredietbank, Brussel
Kredietbank, Gent
Ministerie van Buitenlandse Zaken
Ministerie van Ontwikkelingssamenwerking
Museum Mayer van den Bergh
Nationaal Fonds voor Wetenschappelijk Onderzoek
Nationale Bank van België
Nationiale Dienst voor Afzet van Land- en Tuinbouwprodukten
Nationale Loterij
Openluchtmuseum Bokrijk
Paribas Bank, Leuven
Petrofina
Philips België
Private Kas Bank, Brussel
Province de Liège
Provincie Limburg
Regering van de Vlaamse Gemeenschap
Royale Belge
Sabena World Airlines
Stad Leuven
Stella Artois
Stichting Amici Almae Matris
Stichting Nicolaas Rockox
Superclub
Tiense Bank, Leuven
UNESCO
Vereniging voor het behoud en de valorisatie van de Belgische Industriële Archieven